TELESALES COACHING

Also by the Author

Direct Line to Profits: The Canadian Guide to Telemarketing

Profiting by Phone: No Nonsense Skills and Techniques for Selling and Getting Leads by Telephone

Add-On Selling: How to Squeeze Every Ounce of Potential from Your Sales Calls

TELESALES COACHING

The Ultimate Guide to Helping Your Inside Sales Team
Sell Smarter, Sell Better and Sell MORE

JIM DOMANSKI

Order this book online at www.trafford.com
or email orders@trafford.com

Most Trafford titles are also available at major online book retailers.

Printed in the United States of America.

ISBN: 978-1-4669-5179-2 (sc)
ISBN: 978-1-4669-5180-8 (hc)
ISBN: 978-1-4669-5178-5 (e)

Library of Congress Control Number: 2012914453

Trafford rev. 10/01/2012

 www.trafford.com

North America & international
toll-free: 1 888 232 4444 (USA & Canada)
phone: 250 383 6864 ◆ fax: 812 355 4082

Contents

Dedicated to five great coaches—

Jack Hedman

Paul Graff

Frank Acolina

George Nichols

Art Sobczak

FOREWORD

In my over 30 years in inside sales I have seen lots of changes that have raised the status of inside sales from the lowly-regarded, minimally-compensated telemarketer, to today's Inside Sales Professional, who performs the same role as outside sales, is highly respected, and paid accordingly.

Yes, technology, the marketplace, and a new generation have transformed inside sales. But one thing has not changed, and it never will: the people.

Actually, let me correct myself; if anything, we are living in an environment that is less people-*oriented*, and this includes inside sales. Despite that we supposedly are "more connected" than ever with all of our social media outlets and mobile devices that make us instantly and constantly accessible, we are actually **less** connected when it comes to one-on-one meaningful personal interaction. This is troubling when it comes to managing inside sales pros.

A trend that I have seen over the years is managers and supervisors "managing by metrics," meaning that they read their reports behind closed doors, look at calls-per-hour, contacts, talk time and other measures of *activity* and then implore their reps to "get those numbers up."

I compare that to an athletic coach in any sport simply reading the box score of the previous game—without watching it—and then telling his team, "Let's get that score up this game!"

The primary key to success in inside sales—and outside sales for that matter—is the performance of the people. If no one is working hands on with the players on how to improve, and motivating them to do so, the sales reps' performance will not improve, and will in fact, get worse. Ask any truly great athletic coach and he or she will tell you their function is not to win, but to develop and get the most out of their players. The same is true with sales pros.

And to help you do that, there is no one more qualified and skilled than Jim Domanski.

I've known Jim since both of our early days in the business. When I first met him I was so impressed that I invited him to write a column for my *Telephone Prospecting and Selling Report* newsletter, which he has been doing for over 25 years now.

But, longevity in doing anything doesn't necessarily mean excellence. Except in Jim's case. I am always amazed, but not surprised, at Jim's creativity, insight, and ability to transfer his knowledge in an understandable way that motivates people to USE it. As you will soon discover, he is a regular down-to-earth guy with a great sense of humor and wit, and that will help you relate to him and his message.

Jim flat out knows the strategy, processes, and tactics when it comes to coaching and developing sales pros. In this book, he holds nothing back as he shares the instantly-useable how-to's which will help you to take your sales reps to the next level. Regardless of whether you are a seasoned veteran, or a newly-promoted sales rep who is now managing your former peers, you will find a treasure chest of proven methods in this book.

Everyone needs coaches to help them become better. You've made precisely the right choice in getting on Jim's team to help you help **your** team perform at the highest level possible.

To your coaching success,

Art Sobczak
President, Business By Phone Inc.
Author of many inside sales training books, audios, videos, and more.
www.BusinessByPhone.com
www.SmartCalling.com

INTRODUCTION

The Coaching Solution:
Everything You Need to Know
about Coaching

What This Book Is About

In a nutshell, this is a no-nonsense book on how to increase sales and revenues for your inside telephone sales department or company. Period.

It's a book about the practical and proven process of helping your business-to-business (B2B) telephone reps sell smarter, sell better, and sell more products and services. (Note: the same coaching principles apply to consumer telephone reps as well as field sales reps, too!)

Also, this book is about effectively implementing a coaching program that helps your telesales team modify and improve its selling behavior.

Who Should Read This Book

This book is for anyone who is responsible for directly generating sales from a telesales team. Typically, this might be a B2B telesales manager or supervisor.

Sales trainers would significantly benefit from this book as well.

In addition, this book might be of some value to business owners or sales executives because it shows how utterly simple it is to implement a coaching program that will ultimately improve sales and revenues.

Finally, the book would be of value for *anyone* who has employees who require coaching. While the specific techniques might vary the principles are essentially the same.

The #1 Reason Your Reps Don't Sell More of Your Products or Services

Here's the single biggest reason your inside telephone reps don't sell more. Are you ready for it?

They are not good at selling.

What I mean is that they do not have the fundamental skills and techniques that you'd think they should have mastered. For instance, any of the following may occur:

- They change their opening statements for prospects with each and every call; there is no consistency and no mastery.
- Their opening statements lack a benefit for the prospect.

- They collapse like a house of cards when the client says, "I'm in a meeting." They murmur a sheepish apology for interrupting and stutter some inane response such as, "Er . . . ah . . . when . . . ah . . . is a better time to call?"
- Their qualifying questions are ineffective or nonexistent.
- Their needs analysis consist of three or four closed-ended questions that solicit very little from the client.
- Their pitches are a long-winded stream of consciousness rather than a concise, benefit-oriented sales message.
- Their responses to smokescreen objections (such as "E-mail me something," or "Call me in a couple of weeks") are meek and mild.
- Their closing techniques are nonexistent or inconsistent.

Sound familiar?

It's probably why you have read this far. If it isn't familiar, then you and your telesales reps have everything figured out, and you don't need this book.

But I am willing to bet dollars to donuts that you know precisely what I am talking about. The fact of the matter is that the majority of telesales reps don't apply the skills they have learned. Consequently, when they are dealing with customers or prospects, they don't bring their A game. They bring their B game or worse.

Why? This is no great mystery.

Your reps forget.

They ignore.

They dilute.

They omit.

They apply selling skills incorrectly.

They apply selling skills inconsistently.

They get complacent. Or worse, they get lazy.

But what makes it tragic is most of them don't even know it. They are oblivious to the fact they don't sell well. This doesn't make them bad sales people. This does not make them hopeless. It makes them human. Selling is not easy.

Here's a cold, hard fact: most telesales reps only sell well enough to get by.

They get by for two reasons. First, they work hard. They dial hard and long, and sooner or later, they find a person who wants to buy. What's that old expression? Even a blind squirrel finds a nut. Don't get me wrong; working hard is an admirable trait. Selling is hard work. But hard work is not always smart work. Your reps don't sell more because they don't sell smart. So they get by.

The second reason your reps get by is that clients and prospects are relatively smart and intuitive. If the clients' needs are strong enough, they will buy what you're selling. Maybe you have a great product or service. Maybe you have a heck of a price. Again, in this case, the clients will convince themselves to buy without much prodding. The telesales rep simply facilitates the process. This is particularly true when you have an existing customer base that buys your products regularly. The rep contributes little more than a perfunctory role.

Oh sure, product knowledge is important. That's a given. And there's no question that experience plays a role. But at the end of the day, if you truly monitor your reps and listen to their calls, you will know I am right, and you'll get that vague and uneasy feeling that the reps just don't sell well.

It's all the more frightening—or disappointing—because you may have spent a good deal of time and money on skills training, and the investment isn't panning out. You probably spent a month or two working on a fantastic compensation plan designed to stimulate and motivate the rep . . . but that isn't panning out either.

And that's what this book is about.

It's about improving your reps' performances so that they are using and applying their selling skills more consistently. It's about helping them change and modify their selling behavior by helping them to use what they've got. It's about selling smarter by acting as a conscience, a cheerleader, and a coach.

What to Expect from This Book

If you're expecting scintillating and in-depth processes and methodologies about coaching, then this book is *not* for you.

I don't have secret, *Da Vinci Code*-like systems that I reveal in a glorious manner. I assure you, you won't be left gasping in awe. I am not a social scientist who delves into the bewildering and mysterious world of human motivation and learning. There are people with minds far more brilliant than mine who can tackle those issues. They're much wiser than I am, and I encourage you to read and get their perceptions.

If you're looking for the latest highfalutin trend in coaching, you might be disappointed because there is nothing fancy or sophisticated in this book.

What this book provides is a simple and easy—yes, easy—approach to coaching. It uses common sense and draws on almost twenty years of working with hundreds of telesales reps and dozens of telesales managers, supervisors, trainers, and coaches who must produce sales results.

Skills, desire, aptitude, and knowledge

At some point, I began to clue into the fact that the majority of telesales reps were not doing the best they could do simply because they were not applying what they learned in training. They were not using the selling skills in an effective manner, and they were not getting sales results. It was sort of like being on diet but still ploughing down cheesecake after every meal. The plan was *not* being followed.

There were some reps who simply lacked motivation—drive, desire, and attitude. Motivation is like a pilot light. If it isn't already burning, it's pretty hard to ignite it.

I learned quickly that you can't motivate your reps; your reps motivate themselves.

The best you can do is to create a motivating environment in which coaching plays a part.

There are also reps who—despite a strong desire and motivation—lack the fundamental aptitude. They just don't have the natural ability to sell. Through no fault of their own, telephone sales just isn't the right fit. Kind of like me with golf. I want to play well; I've worked hard at it, but it's not a God-given talent for me. I'll never be good at it, even with coaching.

Finally, knowledge is a third factor that affects selling success. Depending on the complexity of the sale, the more knowledge a rep acquires, the better he or she sells. If a rep can't absorb and apply the knowledge that time and experience brings, then the success rate is impacted.

But when you put those three issues aside and get down to nuts and bolts, most telesales reps are not using their selling skills, techniques, processes, tips, and tactics. Or they are not using them well or consistently.

The trick is to get them to apply what they have learned on a consistent basis. They need to master selling skills.

Change—the real culprit

Seems simply enough, right?

But it's not on account of one single reason.

Change.

Most telesales reps—oh heck, most everyone—resists change. Change is uncomfortable. It's awkward. It makes us feel self-conscious. It's a pebble in a shoe. It chaffs and annoys. It causes us to stumble. Even if the change is for the good, we agonize over it. We resist it. Every fiber in our body says, "Go back! Go back to where it was comfortable, albeit unsuccessful."

A coach is nothing more than someone who helps make change easier, more palatable. Coaching helps the rep over that awkward hump of learning and applying or reapplying skill sets. Coaching modifies behavior. It keeps change on track until it becomes a new habit.

I don't think this is rocket science, do you?

Skills and skills only

So what this book focuses on is how to get your reps to use their selling skills effectively.

This book shows you how to coach your reps to develop their skills and abilities. It reinforces the playbook on selling.

It is a narrow, but critical, focus. If your reps can't sell, then desire, aptitude, and knowledge don't really matter, do they? I have seen reps with plenty of desire fail because they cannot question and qualify or because their sales messages stink or because they wilt when confronted with an objection.

I have watched hard workers fail because hard work without smart works wears thin. Reps burnout. You know this as well as I do. Simply playing the numbers game will slam your reps into a brick wall.

And heaven knows I have seen plenty of knowledge experts fall flat on their faces. The information technology profession is littered with subject matter experts who could not convert their knowledge into meaningful sales messages.

So, if your reps don't have the skill sets, the odds that they'll become effective and successful diminish significantly.

CHAPTER ONE

The Coaching Solution

In this chapter:

- Coaching Defined—Sing from the Same Songbook
- A 4-Step Guide to How Coaching Really Works
- Why Coach? 7 Compelling Reasons to Get Up from Your Desk, Get on the Floor, and Coach Your Telesales Reps
- Coaching Myths and Legends—7 Things Coaching Definitely Is *Not*
- The #1 Reason Why Companies and Managers Don't Coach
- What's Your Excuse? 5 More Reasons Why Managers Don't Coach
- The #1 Reason Why Coaching Programs Fail <u>after</u> They've Been Implemented
- The Top 11 Traits of a Great Telesales Coach
- Is Coaching the Miracle Cure for All Telesales Reps?

Coaching Defined—Sing from the Same Songbook

There are a good many interpretations and definitions of coaching. Let's make certain that we are singing from the same songbook right off the bat. It's vital to understand precisely what coaching is. If I can win your hearts and minds right here and right now, then coaching is a walk in the park.

Definitions

Let's start with a basic definition.

Coaching is the process of helping reps sell smarter, sell better, and sell more.

It doesn't get much simpler than that. Coaching is a benefit-laden process. The words that should catch your eye are "sell smarter," "better," and "more" because those are the precise goals and outcomes of coaching if it's implemented correctly.

If you want to add a little meat to the definition, here's another angle.

Coaching is a way, a process, of helping your telesales reps sell more of your products and services by supporting, encouraging, and assisting them to sell more effectively.

This explanation adds another layer to the definition. Of particular note, the words "supporting, encouraging, and assisting" should jump out at you because that's what coaching is all about.

Adding another layer, the following definition provides a behavior-modification component that the previous two do not.

Coaching is a 4-Step process of setting sales-skills standards, monitoring or observing the telesales reps, analyzing their selling behaviors against those standards, and providing feedback in order to modify or change their behaviors to obtain positive results.

While somewhat more technical, this definition has one major component that the other two do not clearly delineate. This definition talks about modifying or changing the behaviors of the telesales reps.

The challenge of change

Bottom line? The power of coaching is that it can help your telesales reps change.

For telesales reps—or any sales reps—to get better at selling, typically they need to incorporate new skills, techniques, knowledge, processes, and methods. This is what training is all about: providing the skills and techniques to sell better.

It seems easy enough, but actually adopting these new skills is the tough part. Most reps resist change not because they are rebellious, but because they are human. It is human nature to resist change because change is usually uncomfortable, a least for a while.

When something is uncomfortable, we tend to avoid it, resist it, ignore it, and pretend it doesn't exist. But, here's the thing: we tend to go back to the old habits we had. Even if the old habits are ineffective, or the results are mediocre (or poor), many reps would rather feel comfortable than deal with the challenge and discomfort of change at the expense of becoming highly successful or highly paid.

Shocking isn't it? But it explains a lot about human behavior. It explains why training by itself rarely accomplishes much. It explains why great compensation plans don't seem to motivate to the degree we think they should. It explains why most reps linger in the middle of the pack or near the end.

So, if we know change is hard, it's up to us as managers, executives, and business owners to help make the transition easier from one skill set to another. It's up to us to help the reps change their behaviors so that they will be successful. If we don't, most will falter on their own. We should do this not simply for the sake of the poor telesales rep, but also for the improved sales results we are seeking.

Don't be afraid to be selfish here. Coach to help reps achieve the sales results you and your bosses want to see.

A 4-Step Guide to How Coaching Really Works

Telesales coaching is a process, a repeatable event consisting of clearly defined steps or components that can be defined and mastered with time and practice. The good news is that the process never changes. It is like riding a bike; once you've learned it, you'll never forget it. It becomes automatic.

There are four fundamental components to an effective coaching process. They are:

1. Establish the standards.
2. Monitor the calls and the reps.
3. Analyze what you have seen and heard.
4. Provide feedback.

The Telesales Coaching Model

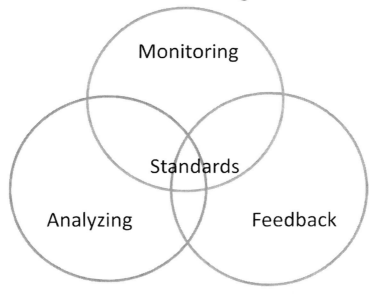

The remainder of the book will delve into these components in detail, but for the moment, here is an overview of each.

Standards

Perhaps the single most important concept of the coaching process is the standard. A standard consists of one or all of the following:

- A set of expectations
- Clearly defined guidelines
- An objective set of steps
- A specific way of doing something
- Something established for use as a rule or a basis of comparison or measurement

Please excuse the multiple definitions, but the standard is vital to the process of telesales coaching, and if there is a secret to good coaching, the standard is it. In the plainest of terms, you cannot coach a skill or technique if a standard has not been set.

To illustrate, here are a couple of examples.

In my telesales training workshops, we discuss that an effective, opening statement for prospecting should include five components.

1. A statement of the rep's full name
2. A statement of the rep's company name
3. The reasons for the call
4. The benefit the prospect/client might derive
5. A bridge to a question

These five parts create the standard by which the coach judges that portion of the call. Sales managers coach to these five parts and these five parts alone. Why? Because that is what the sales reps are taught in training. Coaching reinforces the skills (standards) that were taught.

These steps become the objective measure by which to monitor the call and provide feedback. If the telesales rep nails all five of these elements when being monitored, he or she is selling to-standard. That is, the rep is doing the right things. If he or she misses one of the elements, then the opening statement isn't to-standard, and coaching is required.

Here's another example. Again, in my sales training, there is a simple 3-step process for handling knee-jerk objections, such as "I'm in a meeting." The three steps are:

1. Empathize.
2. Ignore the objection.
3. Ask a question.

If you have a different way of handling this objection or a different way of opening a call, no problem; use it. The beauty of the standard is that it can be whatever you like, as long as it is clearly defined, taught, and supported. Assuming the telesales reps have been taught this process, you can coach to it until the reps have mastered it. If the reps don't empathize, or if they launch into a rebuttal rather than ask a question, you can provide feedback to help them remember and use the process. That's what coaching is.

Implications

To make coaching work, you need to define with precision those skills and techniques that you want your reps to use. If you do *not* do this, if your expectations are vague and unclear, your coaching will be subjective and inconsistent. Your reps will resist the coaching process if your feedback is based on a series of personal and ever-changing tips and tactics. So, if your feedback is not solidly grounded in a standard, your rep will be confused.

What this really means is that you have your work cut out for you. You need to define your sales model, identify the standards, and break them down into steps. After you have taught them in a formal setting, you need to coach those standards diligently.

You know as well as I do that selling requires flexibility and that a standard cannot be set for every single situation. But large portions of your sales model can and should be defined because those parts will be used regularly and consistently. Some skills that can be standardized include:

- Making an opening statement
- Getting past gatekeepers and knee-jerk objections
- Presenting an offer

- Dealing with smokescreen objections
- Asking key qualifying questions
- Leaving a proper voice mail
- Closing a sale
- Up-selling and cross-selling
- Asking for a referral

Monitoring

Monitoring is easy to grasp once you've got a standard.

Monitoring is the process of listening and observing a telesales rep's level of selling relative to a given standard.

As a sales manager, this means you must listen to live or recorded calls and determine if the skills and techniques used by the rep were to the standard taught in training. The point here is obvious; before you can provide any feedback, you need to hear (and sometimes observe) a series of calls.

How, when, and who you monitor will be discussed in later chapters, but for the moment, that's all there is to it.

Analyzing

Analyzing is defined as the process of determining if the telesales rep is performing to the established standards and what if any action is required based on the analysis.

So, if monitoring is the act of listening, then analyzing is the act of determining if the rep is actually using the skills and techniques (i.e., the standards) that were taught. Analyzing is thinking about what you have heard. During analysis, one of three outcomes will become evident.

1. **The call or technique is to-standard.** For example, you monitor your telesales rep, and the opening statement contains the five steps that were taught in training. You listen and hear that they were presented correctly. They were to the standard you set. *Et voila*! The opening is to-standard, so no feedback is necessary for that part of the call.

2. **The call or the technique is not to-standard.** Carrying on from the above, you listen to the call, and for example, the rep encounters a knee-jerk objection. The prospect says, "I'm in a meeting right now." Slightly panicked, your reps blurts out, "Oh, sorry that I interrupted. When would be a better time to call?"

    At this stage your analysis reveals that the handling of the objection was not to-standard. The standard for handling the objection was to empathize, ignore, and ask a question. Based on this analysis, you know that it is necessary to provide feedback in order for the rep to modify the behavior.

3. **The call or the technique is above standard.** This occurs when the sales rep's selling performance is above-standard. This usually means the sales rep not only applied the standard that you set, but also he or she has added a creative or unique twist to the technique, making it even better and more effective.

For example, suppose your monitoring and analysis reveals that the rep provided the 3-step process for pitching the product and added a metaphor to illustrate the benefit. The metaphor was not taught as a standard, but it certainly supplemented the effort.

Here is an opportunity to provide positive feedback. Your analysis revealed the rep has taken the standard to a higher level. You want him or her to continue that behavior, so you'll continue to provide positive feedback.

Feedback

Feedback is the final step in the coaching process. **Defined, feedback is the process used to recognize above-standard and below-standard performance as well as the steps taken to encourage, modify, or improve the selling behavior.**

You will give feedback when you meet with the rep and verbally provide comments, suggestions, corrections, encouragement, and praise. It occurs only after you have monitored and analyzed what you've heard.

Note that feedback applies only to above—and below-standard situations. Unless the skills have just been learned by the telesales rep, feedback is not given for standard performance because, by definition, a standard performance meets the basic expectation.

I will write more on this later, but for now, understand that in the early stages of learning, feedback for standard behavior can and should be given in order to encourage the rep to continue to use the skill or technique. However, after a skill has been mastered, feedback is not required. Many mangers make the mistake of patting their reps on their shoulders when they perform the basic fundamentals. This is unnecessary and risky. Reps will often see this as pandering, and the coaching process can become diluted. If the sales rep becomes cynical of your coaching style, the coaching process will have lost its power.

Why Coach? 7 Compelling Reasons to Get Up from Your Desk, Get on the Floor, and Coach Your Telesales Reps

If you've read this far into the book, you probably have some pretty good reasons for why you think coaching might help you get the most out of your reps. But just in case you need to quantify the issue, here are seven reasons why you should make time to implement a coaching program.

1.   Training is not enough

Training begins the formal process of learning. It imparts the knowledge necessary for the reps to sell. Whether it is related to knowledge, technology, or skills, training is vital. But here's the thing you'll want to guard against; it's called homeostasis.

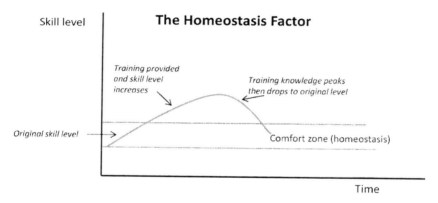

Homeostasis is the tendency for something to go back to a pre-existing comfort zone. For example, have you ever been on a diet and lost a few pounds? What happens to those lost pounds over time? If you are like most people, you gain them back. You know why? Because we all tend to go back to our old eating habits. That's homeostasis at work.

Training usually means change. In selling-skills training, the rep may learn a new way to handle an objection or a new method of asking for a referral. It's different from what the rep has learned in the past. She or he has to change to make it work, and change, whether big or small, tends to be a challenge for the majority of people. So too with your telesales reps. After they have been trained, and no matter how enthusiastic they are, there is some sort of inner switch that tends to pull them back to their old behaviors; homeostasis kicks in.

Enter coaching. Coaching develops and reinforces the skill and ensures that knowledge is applied and used. It encourages the reps to use what they have learned before they give way to homeostasis. Coaching acts as a reminder. It corrects deviations. It encourages. It keeps them on the right track and prevents them from drifting from the skill set or knowledge base.

2. It improves retention

Here's the rational: if you develop the skill and ability of your reps, and they succeed at selling, they will be happy. Call it good morale. If they are successful and content because their needs are being met, they don't usually jump ship. This does two things for you. First, it ensures that sales continue to flow. That makes everyone happy. Second, it reduces costs because turnover stays low. Costs impact margin and profitability. Keeping your reps means spending less time and money recruiting, selecting, hiring, and training replacements. Your boss will love you. You'll look like a hero.

3. It attracts good candidates

When implemented well, a coaching program is like a magnet. It draws good people to your firm. Almost miraculously, better candidates begin to knock at your door because they want to be associated with a company that develops the skills and abilities of their reps. Your existing employees will tell their friends, and they will become instant recruiting agents. This means you can grow your company and your revenues. Again, you're the hero. If you do have turnover, no fears; the pool of applicants will be pretty good.

4.   Carrots are not enough

There are companies and managers who truly believe that if you dangle a big enough carrot, sales reps will perform and succeed. Regrettably, the sales field is littered with discouraged sales reps who tried hard but failed.

Here's the fundamental problem with so-called carrots (contests, incentives, big commissions, etc.): they can get your reps to work harder for a period of time. But what they don't do is teach your reps to work *smarter*. Working hard is good and important. Elbow grease is part of the sales game. But shear hard work can still frustrate and discourage reps when they fail to get the sale.

Coaching teaches reps to combine a strong work ethic with smart work. If they learn and apply the techniques, they'll succeed in taking home the carrot.

5.   Sales experience is not enough

Believe it or not, there are some companies who genuinely feel that hiring an experienced telesales rep is a strategy to sales success. Therein lies an assumption that hiring an experienced rep means that the company does not need to provide comprehensive training and that the rep can hit the ground running.

Do I need to elaborate on this one? Sales experience is no guarantee that the telesales rep will succeed at selling your product to your markets. If the rep does succeed without your intervention, great! You won! You picked the right horse! Congratulations.

But if the rep doesn't succeed like you had hoped, you'd better have something in your hip pocket to salvage the situation. Coaching is the answer. Your new hire might simply need a slight adjustment or two. Make sure you have it.

6. It helps reveal poor performers

Have you ever kept a sales rep on the payroll for too long?

You know who I mean: the rep who was always on the verge of making his or her numbers. You gave that rep a little more time because you sensed he or she was about to break out and sell like crazy. You watched the rep surge a bit, so you gave him or her some more time. But despite all the time you gave and all the potential that he or she seemed to have, you woke up one morning several months or a year down the line, and you realized he or she just wasn't going to cut it.

Usually this sudden realization is followed by the even more overwhelming recognition that you should have probably let this rep go six or eight months earlier. So there you sit and think of the sales opportunities wasted, and you are flooded by guilt and frustration. Sound familiar? Join the crowd.

But it doesn't have to be that way any longer. Coaching would have nipped this situation in the bud. If you had consistently applied coaching to this underachiever, you would have recognized a lot earlier that no amount of watering was going to revive this dead plant.

Coaching quickly sheds light on those who cannot learn and adapt. It tells you that the best choice for you, your company, and the telesales rep is to let the rep go. And if you truly worked at coaching this rep, you could hold your head high with dignity, knowing that you did all you could possibly do. You'd know it was the right time to part ways.

7.   Coaching works

What's the number one reason you should coach your telesales team? It works.

In my twenty or so years of working in B2B telesales, nothing—and I mean nothing—has resulted in better sales results than active coaching. Nothing!

Think about it. Coaching works at getting your telesales reps to modify and adapt their behavior so that they get better at selling. As indicated above, it helps them sell smarter. More importantly, it ensures that they *continue* to sell smarter as opposed to lapsing back into old, less successful behaviors. Coaching is not a short-term Band-aid. It's a long-term program for better sales.

Coaching Myths and Legends—6 Things Coaching Definitely Is *Not*

By clearing defining what coaching isn't, you can better understand the importance of coaching as a means to achieving superior telesales results.

1.   Coaching is *not* a personal anecdote.

I'm sure you've had managers whose approach to coaching was to tell you their war stories from their days in the sales trenches. They dredged up all sorts of colorful anecdotes about how they tackled this objection or that objection, about the flawless presentations, about the countless hours they spent preparing, and of their ability to close on a dime and make the sale.

While some of the good ol' days anecdotes may be interesting, they cannot be mistaken for coaching. The stories might provide a useful tip or two. They might even illustrate a point, which may have a degree of value. But as an effective means to modify and change selling behavior, the stories have limited value.

Why?

First of all, they are often of questionable relevance. Anecdotes tell of a different product, a different time (maybe even a different era), a different market, and a different customer. Somehow, the telesales rep on the receiving end of the anecdote has to extrapolate the similarities to the present—if there are any—and apply them to the situation.

Second, personal anecdotes are not based on an objective standard. This means they cannot be used in a consistent manner. One rep might have one interpretation of the story, while another rep may see it in a wholly different way. As a means of modifying behavior, anecdotes only have validity if they support a technique or skill that has already been taught.

2.   Coaching is *not "rah, rah, sis, boom, bah."*

Coaching is not a Vince Lombardi-like locker-room speech. You see this type of coaching style in managers who are ex-athletes. They act as cheerleaders trying to pump up their reps, get them hyped, and excite them into selling more.

A good speech can help create a motivating environment. A good speech can possibly get a rep to push a little harder and make a few more dials. But however inspirational a speech might be, it does not teach a rep to sell smarter or more effectively. It does not modify or change skill sets.

3. Coaching is *not* training.

A good training program is like a good foundation for a house. The better the foundation, the more you can build and expand. Training is the formal presentation of knowledge. Training is the basis for coaching. If done properly, skills training should set the standards for all parts of the call.

But training is not coaching. Coaching is the process of supporting what was learned in training. If your reps learn how to create an effective opening statement using a 5-step process, coaching should support those five steps. Coaching helps remind the rep to use the steps. It encourages the reps to stick to the plan.

Coaching takes a few seconds—maybe a couple of minutes. Training can take hours.

4. Coaching is *not* an open-door policy.

Some managers think that coaching is telling your reps, "If you're having a problem, come and see me. My door is always open."

That's nice, but it's a cop-out. Sure, some telesales reps will knock on the door and say, "Boss, I need your help." But many, if not most, won't. Some won't because they don't want the embarrassment of saying, "I don't know how to close."

Others, and this is the tragic part, won't rush to the door for help simply because they don't know they need help. Blithely, they go on calling without realizing that they have strayed from the set processes and standards until one day when, being so far behind in their sales objectives, they give up or you give up on them.

Coaching is proactive. It means you actively work with your reps, ensuring that the skills and techniques are being used. It means you pre-empt any problems or difficulties.

5.   Coaching is *not* a personnel review.

Personnel reviews are formal meetings between the manager and the telesales rep. Ostensibly, they are used to provide feedback to the rep on how he or she is doing, what he or she needs to be doing, and so forth. Waiting until a personnel review to give feedback is kind of like closing the barn door after the cows have wandered off.

As a communications process, personnel reviews are great, but they are not the forum for coaching. If the sales rep is stumbling over objections at the beginning of June, you shouldn't wait until the thirtieth to address the issue.

6.   Coaching is *not* a group meeting.

I have worked with several clients who claim that their morning get-together is their means of coaching. They use the time to share techniques, tips, and suggestions. Problems are dealt with. An idea or two is bounced around.

These meetings are great for communicating. Undoubtedly, there is a nugget or two of wisdom. But those kernels of wisdom don't always apply to everyone. And that's the problem; it isn't always applicable.

Coaching is a one-on-one process between you and the rep. A group session might be training, but it is not coaching.

Please don't misunderstand: these six items play a role in disseminating information and imparting knowledge. A good story can illustrate a point and a good speech can motivate a rep to use a technique or a skill. Similarly, reps should know they can come to your door at any time, and any feedback can be of value. But these situations are not a consistent nor an effective means of getting reps to change and modify their behaviors for better results.

The #1 Reason Why Companies and Managers Don't Coach

Do you know the primary reason why companies say they don't coach?

They say they don't have the time. Here's the truth: they think they don't have the time, but they have all the time they need. What they don't have is sense of perspective, and they don't have their priorities straight.

This section addresses the whole, silly notion that managers don't have the time to coach.

No time

Let's begin with the job title of a sales manager. Right off the bat, the implication is that sales managers *manage*. So true. They're busy managing a dozen or more activities: attending meetings, working on spreadsheets, measuring objectives, developing plans, working on projects, dealing with absenteeism, solving problems, attending to the boss, drafting a super presentation, handling customer issues, playing politics with other departments, implementing an incentive plan or sales contest, recruiting and training new inside sales reps, responding to e-mails, putting out fires, approving pricing, and the list goes on.

Whew! I'm exhausted just writing about it. Managers can barely manage being managers! (Couldn't resist.) So, it is not surprising when telesales managers say they don't have time to coach.

To a certain extent, they're right. Coaching—good coaching—does take time. Depending on the sales reps and the situation within a telesales team, initially coaching can and should take about 40 percent to 60 percent of a sales manager's time. Once fully implemented and part of the everyday culture of the department, coaching should still occupy 20 percent of a telesales manager's day. We're talking anywhere from over an hour to as much as five hours in a day.

At this precise moment, I can envision the average sales manager gasping for breath and reaching for an oxygen mask. Most are overwhelmed and shocked by the thought that several hours might have to be spent in the trenches.

Important, but not urgent

Unfortunately for everyone (particularly telesales reps), coaching is one of those "important but not urgent" tasks that management gurus like Stephen Covey and Peter Drucker talk about. If you really want to implement coaching in your organization, it's important to get these terms straight.

Covey, the author of *The 7 Habits of Highly Effective People*, tells us that urgent means something requiring immediate attention. A good example is a ringing phone or an e-mail with a little red exclamation point or memo from the boss asking for input. Often it's an interruption from an employee, a deadline, or a crisis—anything that seemingly demands attention now and forces one to react right away.

"Importance," writes Covey, "has to do with results. If something is important, it contributes to your mission, your values, your high priority goals." (Stephen R. Covey, 1989, page 151). Here's the thing: many important issues are not urgent. They don't have that in-your-face feel about them because they often refer to initiative and pro-activity.

Coaching is a good example of a proactive task. By implementing coaching, your reps will slowly but surely get better at selling and generating revenues. But the act of coaching—sitting down, listening to the call, and providing feedback—is not urgent. It can usually wait. And managers do just that; they put off coaching because something more urgent, though not necessarily more important, comes up.

Management experts will also tell you that there are "urgent but unimportant" activities that steal time away from managers. Think of all those "urgent" meetings you've attended and wondered, *What the heck am I doing here?* Think of those reports that took hours of your time, only to sit, unopened, on your boss's desk. This list goes on.

Perspective

So how do you wrap your head around this issue? How do you make coaching both important and urgent?

Get some perspective. Answer these questions:

⇨ Who plans and organizes the telephone call?
⇨ Who picks up the phone and dials the number?
⇨ Who battles past gatekeepers to reach decision makers?
⇨ Who has to penetrate voice mail and caller ID displays to speak to the prospect?
⇨ Who presents the opening statement that gets the client or prospect to listen?

⇨ Who asks the questions to identify the needs?

⇨ Who presents the appropriate solution?

⇨ Who handles the inevitable objections?

⇨ Who advances the sales cycle?

⇨ Who closes the sale?

⇨ Who cross-sells and up-sells?

⇨ Who generates the revenue?

⇨ Who helps make the margin?

⇨ Whose job is it to meet or exceed his or her sales objective?

⇨ Who can make you look good?

⇨ And who can make you look bad?

The answer to all of these questions is the same: the telesales rep.

The telesales rep is the key to your success because it is the sales reps who bring home the bacon. Without them, without the revenues they produce, nothing else really matters.

Okay, by contrast, consider the answers to this list of questions:

- Does a spreadsheet generate a single dime of revenue?
- How much revenue did your last staff meeting make for the company?
- What was the net margin on that last project?
- How many new customers did the unresolvable issue with the accounting department produce?

Get your priorities right.

There is certainly no question that managers do have to attend meetings, put out fires, deal with the accounting department, and tackle various projects. The issue is priority.

The telesales rep is the conduit for sales, customer growth, revenue, and margin. If your time is not proportionately spent with those who make you the money, then you've got your priorities dead wrong. There is simply no delicate way to put it.

Give your head a shake. Give up a meeting or two. Say no to a project. Skip *American Idol* tonight, and finish up your report at home. Come in early, and study your spreadsheet. I don't care what you do, but make time for those who are going to make *you* successful.

What's Your Excuse? 5 More Reasons Why Companies and Managers Don't Coach

Not all managers say they don't have the time to coach. Here are five more reasons that managers and company owners toss out as their excuses for not coaching.

1.   Our sales reps don't like it.

Put another way, companies will explain that reps don't like coaching because the monitoring of calls is interpreted as spying. Reps will claim that management doesn't trust them. They'll say, "You're trying to catch us doing something wrong."

There may be some truth to these remarks, but there may also may be some side-stepping. Reps don't like coaching for one of two reasons. The first reason is somewhat legitimate. Perhaps, at one time, they were coached and beaten with a big stick. In other words, the coaching was a negative event. For example, often under the guise of quality control, many companies actually rate a call, giving it a score or grading it like a report card. Who likes that?

Weighting parts of a call and then grading them is one of the most negative things you can do in the name of coaching. The trouble with this type of evaluative approach to coaching is that it is extremely subjective. Put five managers in a room, and have them monitor a call using a grading system (such as on a scale of one to five, where one is poor, three is middling, and five is great) and you won't ever see consensus. Never, ever. Reps know this, so how can the rating help? In addition, this approach rarely provides specific feedback for the rep on how to improve the score—how to move from a three to a four, much less to a five.

If your rep came from that sort of environment, his or her dislike of coaching is understandable.

The second reason why reps don't like coaching might be because they know they don't perform well and fear that their mediocrity is going to catch up with them sooner than later. They fear that coaching is going to make it tougher on them. They fear they will get coached and fail.

Whether these fears are legitimate or not, do *not* let them prevent the implementation of a coaching program. Your coaching program—the one based on the information you take from this book—will be a positive process. It will not grade your telesales reps. You will not use a big stick to punish, embarrass, or intimidate your reps. Tell them that.

Coaching is a positive thing because it helps everyone succeed. When they see your patient, persistent, and positive approach to coaching, they'll relax. They'll learn to appreciate and welcome it.

And if your reps still don't like it—tough. Don't let the tail wag the dog. Coaching will help you and your company succeed. If the rep doesn't want to get on board, you might have to consider leaving him at the station.

2.   Our sales managers don't like it.

This excuse for not coaching is different from the excuse mentioned earlier about not having enough time. Managers don't like coaching for three reasons. First, they don't like it because, quite frankly, it can be boring. Monitoring calls, whether recorded or live, while sitting next to the rep or at another desk, can be tedious.

Tough. Get over it. Just do it.

The second reason managers don't like coaching is that they don't know how to do it very well. As such, the coaching they may have provided to their reps in the past probably hasn't produced stellar results. Hence, the perceived value of coaching is often the real objection.

Most managers have never been taught the skills or techniques to be a good coach. They fly by the seat of their pants, they emulate a sports coach, or they wing it. The bottom line is that their efforts are not typically effective.

Once they learn how to coach effectively, they'll see results. And they'll change their minds about coaching.

And the third, most pervasive reason is that managers are like everyone else—they don't like change. Learning how to coach or learning to coach in a different manner means changing behaviors, approaches, and styles. It means having to adapt to new things. We already know change is tough, so just tolerate the discomfort and change anyway.

3.   We don't need to coach; we hire experienced reps.

This is worth a second look because companies that try to justify their lack of coaching use this one a lot. Hiring experienced reps offers no guarantee that they'll produce big-time sales results. If they do, you can laugh at me all the way to the bank. You won't have to coach as you count the cash, and coaching will be a nonissue.

But what happens if the experienced sales reps don't succeed? What's plan B? Hire *more experienced* reps and hope they pan out better?

Plan B is coaching. If your experienced reps are struggling, help them succeed; don't let them fail.

4.   We have a quality control department.

I have never been, nor will I ever be, a big fan of quality control insofar as coaching is concerned. Don't mistake a quality control department for coaching. There are four major reasons why.

First, quality controllers typically monitor recorded calls from another room or floor. It is a rare event to see a quality controller side-by-side with a rep using a Y-jack. While there are certainly benefits to remote monitoring, quality control is more often seen as "watchful big brother" rather than monitoring for coaching purposes.

Second, quality controllers grade calls. They score them. Portions of the call are weighted by importance and then scored to give a figure out of one hundred—kind of like report cards. They are just about as popular, too. As I've mentioned, grading calls is highly, highly subjective. Because it is so subjective, the coaching that results from it is arbitrary at best and does little to modify behavior. Grading is a destructive process when it comes to coaching.

Third, the quality controllers rarely provide the feedback. Usually, some sort of score sheet (the report card) is sent to the manager, who is left with the task of providing feedback. It's like asking someone else to watch your kids and having them tell you if the kids did something wrong, leaving you to address the behavior hours or days after it happened. It abdicates responsibility. The manager may not even agree with the assessment. And the telesales rep is certainly left defenseless.

Finally, more often than not, the feedback, like the monitoring, is provided hours, days, or weeks after the call is monitored. Providing feedback that much time later means the rep has continued with substandard behavior for dozens of calls when it could—and should—have been nipped in the bud.

If you have a quality control department, use it only to identify trends in call quality. If they find a rep who may need feedback, then the manager/coach should monitor that rep's calls. Once the manager is convinced there is substandard performance, feedback can be provided that is objective, relevant, and meaningful.

5.   We don't know how.

Thankfully, this is not an excuse. This is a reason—a legitimate reason. If you don't know how to coach, perhaps you have been avoiding it. That's okay. But ignorance is not bliss. Nor is it excusable.

The good news is you can fix this. Simply read on.

The #1 Reason Why Coaching Programs Fail <u>after</u> They've Been Implemented

Some companies have implemented coaching programs in the past, but they have failed. Do you know the number one cause for that failure?

It's not giving up too soon. That reason probably places second on the list. And it's not poor implementation either. That probably ranks as the number three reason. Nor is it failure due to a lousy manager—although that is a factor from time to time.

Lack of executive support

The primary reason why coaching fails is lack of executive or owner support.

If there is no executive guardian angel supporting the initiative in your company, the coaching program is more or less bound for oblivion. Here's why. Coaching is a philosophy, if you like. You either believe that modifying behavior is a key ingredient to sales success or you don't. Halfway doesn't cut it—never has, never will. If there isn't a buy-in at the top level, sooner or later the coaching program will take a hit.

Many executives or owners only pay lip service to that philosophy. When things get hectic and busy, or when sales take a bit of dip, suddenly coaching is put aside. If the results of the coaching effort are not apparent in a short while, the strategy gets placed on the back burner. If a manager is behind on a project that the executive needs on his desk later in the week, he's told to skip the coaching.

Very quickly, the manager who is responsible for implementing the coaching program learns that it's not a priority for the boss. Guess what happens then? The coaching peters out.

Active buy-in

For coaching to work well at your company, you need executive buy-in and support on an active and ongoing basis. In effect, the executive or the owner must be the coach of the coach. The executive must monitor the coaching of the coach on a fairly regular basis. He or she must act as a conscience at times and as a cheerleader at others. Above all, the executive must hold the coach accountable for managing and implementing the coaching process. That means regular reports and feedback.

Occasionally, the executive or owner must leave the corner office to tour the floor, listen to taped calls, monitor live calls, sit beside the rep, and get a feel for the calls he or she is making. Executives should examine the monitoring sheets from time to time. If the executive shows that the coaching strategy is important, it becomes important. It tells the manager (coach) and the reps that coaching is not just the latest fad that will soon fizzle out. It shows that the approach is here to stay.

Wave the magic wand

If the executive buys in, like a magician waving a wand, your coaching program will work. The myriad reasons why it doesn't work will miraculously disappear into thin air. Presto! For instance, the question about how to find the time to do the coaching will vanish instantly because the manager will know that coaching is both important and urgent. The manager is clear on his priorities. Quitting the coaching program isn't an option when the boss says it isn't an option. Similarly, poor implementation won't be tolerated, especially if there is a consequence for it.

If you're a manager and you want to make sure your boss understands how critical this is, photocopy this section and slip it into his inbox late one night. Use a highlighter for things you think are particularly important. You don't have to sign it—just leave it, and run away. Or if you are real gutsy, hand it to your boss and say, "Hey, what do you think?"

Let me know how it goes.
Write to me at jim@teleconceptsconsulting.com

The Top 11 Traits of a Great Telesales Coach

What makes a good—no, wait—a great telesales coach?

What are the traits that make great coaches more effective than others?

Trait #1: A great coach takes an organized approach and commits to the program.

The best of coaches are organized. This is perhaps one of the most important traits of a great coach because it shows commitment. Great coaches know that the success of their department, and ultimately of the company, is based on their telesales reps. The better the rep, the better the results. Knowing this, they establish a coaching schedule each and every week. They know that coaching is like an exercise program; the more they follow the coaching schedule, the stronger their reps will become.

And this organized and committed approach tells their team that their success is important. They stick to the program because the program produces results.

Trait #2: A great coach adapts a process-oriented consistency.

The actual coaching process with the telesales rep is not arbitrary. It is consistent. The telesales rep understands the coach's methodology, which should include four key components: standards, monitoring, analysis, and feedback.

The great manager consistently monitors a call based on the set of skill standards that were established in the initial training (see "Objectivity" below). The great manager analyzes what she or he hears and provides feedback designed to positively modify or change sales behavior. This is no willy-nilly, shoot-from-the-hip approach to coaching. It is reliable, predictable, and consistent.

Trait #3: A great coach encourages participative feedback.

Great coaches don't tell their rep what they observed or what they did wrong. Great coaches ask questions such as, "Mark, how do you feel that call went?" or "Chantal, relative to what we learned about handling knee-jerk objections, how do you think that call went?" By doing this, the manager is allowing the rep to participate and, in effect, coach himself or herself. This establishes a two-way dialogue, not a one-way monologue. The rep must do the analysis, making it more meaningful and taking the onus off the coach.

Trait #4: A great coach is objective.

Great coaches are objective with their feedback. They eliminate the arbitrary and subjective nature of feedback by clearly defining the standards for certain key parts of a call. For instance, as illustrated earlier, a good opening statement might have five key components that create a standard. Everyone on the floor knows this. When feedback is provided on the opening, it is based on those five components and not on the whim of the coach at that moment. The telesales rep understands this and knows it is not a personal perspective. This makes the feedback meaningful, relevant, and easier to apply.

Trait #5: A great coach is knowledgeable and skilled.

Perhaps it is understood, but great coaches are knowledgeable. They know the products or services. But more significantly, they know the sales process, including the skills and techniques that contribute to success. Selling skills combined with product knowledge create a successful rep.

The more the manager understands these two elements, the better he or she can help the rep improve his or her selling behavior.

Trait #6: A great coach is balanced and fair.

Studies reveal that negative, albeit constructive, feedback is given five times more frequently than positive feedback. A great coach knows this and battles it. A great coach looks for and provides positive feedback. But more importantly, a great coach knows not to dilute the positive with the constructive. (For example, "Laura, that was a really great opening statement. Well done. But your question sequence was weak.") A great coach gives good news and good news only. Great coaches let their reps bathe in praise when it's earned. Or they give constructive feedback and constructive feedback only. There is no mixing of messages and hence, no confusion.

Trait #7: A great coach demonstrates flexibility and is able to adjust.

While a great manager is process oriented and utilizes clearly defined standards to guide the analysis, he or she can be flexible in the manner and tone in which coaching is applied. A great coach adjusts to the personality and behavior of the individual rep. Analytical reps get more structure in their feedback. Driver-type reps get direct, straightforward feedback. Amiable reps are handled with a little more sensitivity. Expressive reps get banter. This means the coach knows—really knows—the rep.

Trait #8: A great coach is patient and tolerant.

Most people resist change even if the change is for the good. Changing and modifying sales behavior takes time and effort. Some reps adjust quickly, some don't. A good coach is aware of that and is patient. Reps will make mistakes, sometimes repeatedly. A good coach is tolerant of mistakes. It may mean a little more extra coaching and a little more time, but often that's what is necessary for success. So he or she hunkers down and gets the job done.

Trait #9: A great coach is tough.

A great coach knows when to be tough and kick butt. This means identifying the reps who consistently underperform and putting them on a "get-well program." It means sticking to creating and communicating clear expectations, putting the reps on a plan, and keeping them on task. It means following up—lots of following up. It means not falling for excuses, and it means not extending deadline after deadline. It's tough love.

Trait #10: A great coach is realistic.

A great coach is realistic. Great coaches know when the coaching is *not* working and get-well programs have not succeeded. It means letting go—terminating. The key point is this: for whatever reason, not every rep will benefit from coaching efforts. Some reps will not apply the skills or techniques and won't succeed. Great coaches know when to quit. They know when to move on. They know that it is better to work on those who can grow than those who won't.

Trait #11: A great coach is a good communicator.

I suppose it goes without saying, but a great coach is a great communicator. He or she is able to provide feedback in a manner that is clear and easy to understand. Maybe this is the most important trait because if you can't effectively articulate your observations and feedback, the rest of the traits don't matter quite as much, do they?

Of course communication is a two-way street. On the one hand, a good communicator is a good listener. A good coach listens and evaluates what the telesales rep has to say when feedback is being provided. The great coach acknowledges the rep's comments. On the other hand, a good communicator is also a good conveyer of messages. This is the beauty of having a coaching "process." It can direct and funnel your comments so that they are concise and meaningful. When you have clearly defined standards, your feedback is not vague. It is anchored to specifics. And as you'll see, the primary means of providing feedback is through asking questions and letting the reps do their own self-analyses. This makes you an even better communicator.

The good coach has many of these traits. A great coach has all of them. Being a great coach isn't easy, but nothing great ever comes easily. Work at it. Be a *great* coach.

Is Coaching the Miracle Cure for All Telesales Reps?

Okay, I have raved about coaching and what it can do for your reps, your sales, and your revenues. It would seem it's a miracle cure. It would seem it's the greatest thing since sliced bread, right?

But will it work for *all* of your telesales reps?

No.

Regrettably, coaching does not work with or for everyone on your sales team. In fact, at some point, you'll discover you can group your telesales team into three broad categories: those can be coached, those who can't be coached, and those who won't be coached.

1. Those who can be coached

The majority of your telesales team can be coached and will be receptive to your efforts to varying degrees. Obviously, this is your sweet spot. You like this group because these are the reps who will take you to the promised land of increased revenues and sales success.

There are no hard and fast rules here, but on average, 60 percent to 70 percent of your reps will likely fall into this category. It may be more or less depending on your team. Some will eagerly embrace coaching completely, while others will take to it only partially but enough to make an impact. You can up this percentage by being more rigorous in your selection and hiring process. The more mouldable the recruit, the better the receptivity will be to coaching results.

Obviously, it is here that you want to spend the majority of your time and effort. Depending on the size of your telesales team, you will quickly discover that you can't apply the same level of coaching to everyone all the time. Unless you are a full-time coach, you'll be overwhelmed. So you need to make smart decisions on where and how you spend the effort.

2. Those who can't be coached

It might take a little time, but chances are you'll find that there are reps on your team who simply can't be coached. It is not that they are not receptive to coaching, but rather it is that they can't seem to apply or master the change of behavior.

Here is a simple but apt example. I can't dance a lick. No talent. None. *Nada. Nyet.* I do not have an innate sense of rhythm or beat. I look and feel clumsy. It's not for a lack of trying. I have tried. It's not for a lack of effort. I have learned steps. But I can't seem to apply them with any sort of suaveness or panache. It's frightening to behold.

You'll get that same situation with some of the reps on your team. They can't do the sales dance no matter what you do. They lack the innate talent. And the trouble is, many of them have a good attitude. They have the desire to succeed and improve, but it just doesn't translate to the sales floor. These reps will frustrate and bewilder you because they just can't seem to get it despite your attention, effort, and focus.

Generally, these reps take care of themselves in that they leave on their own accord when they discover they're not succeeding. Others, unfortunately, have to be let go. But the point is that you'll discover that coaching doesn't work because the rep is not wired for sales. It will take you some time, but in the end, you'll realize you have done all you can and that it is time to part ways.

3.   Those who won't be coached

Finally, the most frustrating group of reps are those who won't be coached.

It's not that they can't take feedback and change their behavior, it's that they choose not to. This group is often bright, if not gifted and extremely talented, but they resist the coaching effort.

Superstars

Talented superstars are very typical of this group. They are where they are at because of their own street savvy (or at least, that is what they think). They have their own way of doing things and tend to resist anyone or anything that interferes with their "successful" methods.

Leave them be. Don't mess with their "mojo."

Unless their selling style is unethical or negative, let them sell in their own manner. You will see this farther on in the book, but the bottom-line purpose of this book is to get results. Sales results. If the superstars are getting the results you want, let them be. Oh sure, you might say they could get even better results through the coaching process, and you might be right. But if they fight or otherwise resist you, move on to someone else who really needs your help. Spend your time coaching with those who will most benefit from the effort.

Old Salts

Another group that falls under this category are the old salts (i.e., the savvy veterans who have been around for a while). They might be superstars, but not necessarily so. Their claim to fame is that they have toughed it out for more than a few years. Usually this implies that they have had some sales success; otherwise, they wouldn't be around.

But with some of them (not all), it's a matter of teaching the old dogs some new tricks. If you are not already accustomed to it, some of these reps won't be coached because they choose not to leave their comfort zones. They might be complacent, maybe even lazy.

Of course, give coaching a try. If they respond, great. If not, look at their numbers. Though uninspiring, if the numbers are there, forget about them. It's all about effort and reward. Go where the reward is the greatest.

Embittered

The last group that seems to resist coaching are the embittered reps. These are reps who have chips on their shoulders about something. If you've managed a rep who exhibits this behavior, you will know precisely what I am talking about. They resist your coaching efforts because it is their nature to resist, fight, and complain about nearly everything.

The trouble with the embittered reps is they are often very talented and succeed in getting results. Most managers are torn between tolerating them or tossing them out the door. Most companies keep these reps because results are key.

Fine. But there are three stipulations. First, you can try coaching, but if they throw it in your face, don't bother. It's just not worth it. Second, if they trash talk your coaching efforts with other employees (which they often do), haul them in and have "the talk." And third, if they continue to be a problem relative to your coaching efforts, get rid of them. It's tough, but do it. The embittered can often act like cancer cells and spread throughout your team, infecting others. Or they intimidate others by scoffing at your ideas.

The point of this section was not to discourage you, but rather to give you the straight goods on what you will encounter. It's not all rose blossoms.

Coach those who can be coached. Coach them well. Coach those whom you are not certain about, and then you can determine if they can't be coached or won't be coached. Work from there. You'll be channeling your energies in the proper direction, and you'll get better results because of it.

CHAPTER TWO

Step #1: Establishing Standards

The first step in the coaching process is establishing standards. This means defining precisely what you want to coach as well as the selling behaviors you want your inside sales reps to employ to be more successful at selling.

In this chapter:

- Standards—Revisited and Defined
- What Happens When You Don't Have Standards
- 3 Steps to Creating a Standard
- Troubleshooting: Exceptions to the Standard
- It's Not a Numbers Game—Setting Numeric Standards

Standards—Revisited and Defined

In case you missed it in the first chapter, the standard is perhaps the single most important concept of the coaching process. If this section is a bit repetitive it's because it is worth another mention; it's that vital. Here's the definition once again. A standard consists of one or all of the following:

- A set of expectations
- Clearly defined guidelines
- An objective set of steps
- A specific way of doing something
- Something established for use as a rule or a basis of comparison or measurement

You cannot provide effective feedback as a coach if you have not clearly defined your expectations for certain parts of a call. If you have not set the expectation (aka the standard) for certain key parts of a call, your feedback will be, at best, subjective and anecdotal.

A set of standards forces you to define how you must do something. It forces you to define how your rep should prepare his or her call. It forces you to list the steps required for a good opening statement or how to handle a smokescreen or knee-jerk objection. Once everyone on your team knows the expectations, there are no surprises when it comes to providing feedback. The feedback is based on those precise standards. This makes your feedback objective, fair, and, above all, effective. That's all there is to it.

What Happens When You Don't Have Standards

Let me tell you a little story. It literally occurred just as I sat down to write this section. The phone rang. It was my buddy who owns a call center. He was telling me about their coaching efforts.

"Jim," he says, "my executive team and I were just monitoring some of the calls the reps make, and I have to tell you I was disappointed. The calls lacked professionalism."

I asked him what he meant by "professionalism." Specifically, I inquired about the specific components that make a call professional. At this stage, he began to define professionalism, but he struggled. He could not precisely put his finger on what he expected, but what he heard was not what he wanted. It was one of those maddening "I'll know it when I hear it" moments. How do you train or coach to the unknown?

I had this vision of the managers beseeching the reps: "Be more professional." Then I imagined the bewildered reps desperately trying to figure out precisely what that meant.

Does that sound familiar to you? Does it sound like *you*?

I understood his point. I think he wanted a crisp call that was flawless in delivery, sharp in replies to objections, and smooth in a transition to a close. But these are feelings and intuitions, not steps. You can't coach feelings and intuition.

When you don't have clearly defined standards, and when you don't communicate with your telesales reps, the net result is disappointment. The coaching effort will be diluted and wasted.

If your team does not know what is expected at any stage of a sales call, you can bet you'll get a hodgepodge of techniques and tactics, and they'll be all over the map. Some of what you hear will be pretty darn good, as reps use common sense and past experience to deal with a situation. On the other hand, some of it will be mediocre or lousy and ultimately ineffective.

Subjectivity

Without a standard, your feedback will be subjective at best.

Even if the feedback you provide is particularly good, it may not sustain itself for future calls. That's because the feedback is not grounded against a comparative standard. There is no set structure from which to build the skill set. Moreover, your feedback may be given out of context to the rest of the call. In other words, it is meaningless in the grand scheme of things.

When you tell people what you want and why, they at least know what you expect. If you don't, if you're vague, or if your feedback changes by situation or by rep, you'll create confusion, resentment, and ineffectiveness.

If you don't have standards, you don't have a coaching process. In which case, don't bother any further. Don't monitor the calls and don't provide feedback. It will be fleeting and temporary at best.

3 Steps to Creating a Standard

Have you ever heard of the acronym SOP?

It stands for standard operating procedure. It's a way of indicating how things are done. It's just another way to define standards, and it captures the essence of creating a standard.

To create standards for selling, you simply break down a sales call into its logical parts and define how each part is done. Each of these elements should have an SOP applied to it. That's how you create your standards.

Step #1: Define your selling module.

The first step to identifying and setting your standards is to define your selling model. In the B2B, telesales model below, there are five distinctive components to selling.

The 5-Step Telesales Model

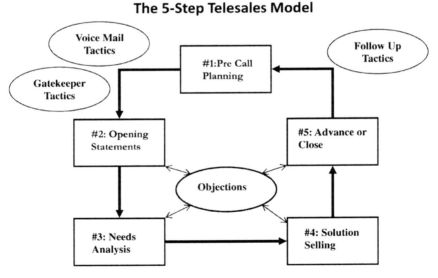

-standards can be established for each of the steps and sub-steps

Right off the bat, you have your first standard. A good call, from start to finish, should have these five components. If you monitor a call and it is missing parts of this, the call is not to-standard and you can provide feedback accordingly. (Please note: common sense must be used here. Not all calls will follow this process. For example, a follow-up call on a proposal might not require a presentation because the proposal covers that aspect of the call.)

Step #2: Define your way of doing things (your SOP) for each component of the call.

Pre-call planning

When I provide a training program, I have a methodology for the planning of a call. The telesales reps are taught to use a pre-call planning sheet that provides a roadmap for the call they are about to make. For example, they must define and write down their primary objective, followed by their secondary objectives.

The sheet also requires the rep to jot down his or her opening statement in either word-for-word format or in point form. This is followed by a section where the rep must note his or her key questions and list key selling points. A final section is reserved for "closing" or "advancing the sale."

The standard for the pre-call planning sheet is that the rep completes a sheet for certain defined calls. If the rep does not complete the sheet, the planning is not to-standard. What that means is that feedback is required to help modify the behavior. The rep needs to be reminded about using the sheet.

Opening statement

Would you agree that an opening statement is one of the most critical components of any telesales call? Of course, who wouldn't? So it makes sense that you have a clearly defined way of opening the call.

In my world of training, there are five components to an effective B2B telesales call. They are:

1. A statement of the rep's full name
2. A statement of the rep's company name
3. The reasons for the call
4. The benefit of the product or service
5. A bridge to a question

Your opening statement for your telesales team may have different components or standards. It doesn't matter. Whatever you decide is the standard operating procedure is okay so long as it is well defined.

In my opening, there is a great deal of room for flexibility on the rep's part. It is not a script, but rather it is a process. When monitoring, I listen for these five steps. They are either there or they are not. It is black and white. If one or more steps are missing, I can objectively coach the reps so that they can master the process.

Note the word "process." The standard is a process, not a word-for-word script. If you want to develop a script and hand it to the reps to use, do so.

Questioning

Unless your sale is very transactional and very scripted, it can be challenging to describe the standards for questioning. When I work with clients, we define what information telesales reps are expected to extract from a client or a prospect. The information becomes the standard. What questions the reps uses to elicit that information is up to the rep.

For example, you might want to know the prospect's company's size or if a budget is available or the volume of widgets shipped. You may also want to find out what they are looking for in a vendor or whether or not the person on the phone is the only decision maker. There are many questions that will uncover this information. Precisely how they uncover it is less important.

The key here is that the rep must know what information is necessary to qualify a prospect or make a sale. The information is the standard.

Your situation may be different. You might have certain key questions that *must* be asked. Good for you. Go for it.

The point is that you took the time and effort to define and communicate those specifics to your rep. By mastering the process, the reps become more successful. That's the whole point.

Presentation

Presentation can be defined in many ways. For our purposes here, presentation is how you present your offer or describe your product or service. You might call it a pitch. A classic process for presentation carries the acronym FEB (feature, explanation, or benefit). This becomes the standard.

So, if your rep is recommending a webinar on personnel evaluation software, the message should clearly explain what the webinar will cover and precisely what benefits the attendee can expect. Within the explanation, there might be three key points your rep should mention. If so, they too become part of the procedure.

You monitor the FEB process, and you monitor the three sub points within the explanation. If the rep covers all the bases, his or her call is to-standard, and that rep will probably start succeeding. If the rep is missing portions here and there, the coach needs to give feedback to remind the rep to stay on track.

Close

I'm sure we can all agree that closing is important. Because it is important and increases sales success, it becomes a standard. There isn't much doubt about that.

There must be fifty ways to close the sale (for example, the direct approach, the assumptive, the alternate choice, the Ben Franklin, the try close, just to name a few). So long as one of them is used, I personally don't care. You might feel differently. The point with my coaching is that the rep attempts a close. This is a standard. (Note, here is where it may become more of an art than a science. There are times when a close simply doesn't apply to a given call. Use your common sense. If you monitor a call and a close could have been applied, provide feedback. If not, fine.)

Other standards

We've looked at a simple sales model. But there are other aspects to a sales call that impact effectiveness. For instance, here are some elements of a call that might benefit from the development of a standard operating procedure:

⇨ **Getting past voice mail**

You might have some techniques that a rep uses to reach a live decision maker before ever leaving a message (such as trying different times, using an internal transfer, calling from a cell phone or a pay phone, etc.).

⇨ **Leaving voice mail messages**

You might have four or five template voice mail messages (I certainly do) that reps can use; they can use any of them but they must use *one* of them.

⇨ **Techniques to sidestep gatekeepers**

I teach nine different techniques to get past a gatekeeper; this gives the rep flexibility and allows him or her to choose a standardized process that fits his or her personality.

⇨ **Handling knee-jerk objections**

You might have a process to handle these kinds of objections, which occur at the beginning of a call. (I have a the aforementioned 3-step process), or you might have scripted responses.

⇨ **Handling smokescreen objections**

You may have a scripted standard or a technique to overcome objections that are tossed out after the call; either way, this is what the rep is to use.

⇨ **Cross-selling**

Provide the rep with a specific methodology of how to sell additional products over and above the original purchase (think McDonalds: "Would you like fries with that?")

⇨ **Up-selling**

Same as cross-selling but selling more of the same product (think McDonalds again: customer orders fries and the rep upgrades the order to "biggie" fries).

⇨ **Referral-gathering techniques**

Give your rep a scripted line or two that creates the standard of precisely how to ask for a referral.

⇨ **Qualifying process**

As discussed above in questioning, you don't have to give them the precise questions, but you might establish the standard that they must determine if the prospect's company has a budget, if the prospect is the decision maker, and if there is a precise time frame for the purchase decision.

If you want, you can create call standards for virtually any repeatable activity. For instance, you could have specific standards for prospecting e-mails. If you think it is important that a rep do it well and consistently, then train your reps on the technique, make it a standard, and coach to it.

Getting started

Okay, it might be fairly obvious that identifying the standards might take some work. If you have a formal telesales training program, creating standards is relatively easy. Use the step-by-step techniques from the training program, and make them the basis of your standard operating procedures.

If you don't have a formal training program, you need to implement one. Without formal training, whereby the standards are communicated to your reps, there is no basis for coaching.

Here's a fast, easy and cost effective way to implement a training program and create a set of selling standards. Art Sobczak, president of Business by Phone (visit: www.businessbyphone.com) has written a superb book on B2B telephone selling entitled *"Smart Calling: Eliminate the Fear, Failure and Rejection from Cold Calling."* Buy this magnificent how-to book and use it as the basis for your training and your standards.

Step #3: Add or delete standards as you go.

Don't get pig-headed about standards; be flexible.

If you create a standard and it doesn't seem to work, or it loses its relevance, get rid of it. If one of your telesales reps develops a process or technique that works exceedingly well, adopt it and make a new standard.

Understand this: standards are not created for the sake of getting reps to comply for compliance's sake.

Standards are created as a basis for coaching and sales improvement. If there are better ways to handle an objection or get past voice mail or cross-sell a product, then steal them, implement them, and coach to them.

If you provide ongoing training throughout the year, keep a close eye on the techniques you feel should be incorporated into the daily selling routine. These become new standards. Communicate these to your reps, and start monitoring for their usage. By doing so, you will protect your training investment because your reps will actually begin to *use* the techniques instead of saying, "Gee, that was nice information; okay, let's get back to our old ways."

Troubleshooting: Exceptions to the Standard

All roads lead to Rome.

And there are many ways to sell. Just because you define the standard for an opening, it doesn't mean there aren't half a dozen other ways that are equally as effective.

You'll get pushback from reps once you establish a standard. Many won't like your way of doing something simply because it is *your* way and not *their* way. Sometimes—maybe even often—their way is very effective. You can run into a good deal of conflict when you define and implement standards, and if you're not prepared for it, you can create chaos. In fact, it could even impact sales success.

Savvy veterans and mavericks

Suppose you have an old veteran on your team—someone who's been with you for a long time and who doesn't sell to the standards that you set. Then what? Here's what you do.

First, look at his or her sales results. If the savvy veteran is cranking out sales and is at 100 percent of quota most of the time, then let him or her be! The standards were created to help you provide feedback that will effectively modify behavior and increase sales. If the sales are already there, you don't have to get your reps to comply for the sake of compliance.

As noted earlier, change is hard. Don't invite unnecessary change. If you're getting what you want, leave your veteran rep alone.

Second, look at his or her processes. If the savvy vet is using a particular good and effective technique, you may want to adapt it as standard as suggested in the section above. More than likely, the veteran has a style that is unique to him or her and is rarely transferable. If that's the case, fine. Leave it alone. The goal is sales. You're getting them.

Third, is he or she behaving ethically? Naturally, any technique or process should be viewed through an ethical lens. Provided the technique is legitimate and does not compromise the integrity of the selling process, it should be okay.

The maverick is simply a variation of the savvy vet. The maverick is the rep who doesn't comply with anything. Apply the same principles. If you are getting sales, leave the maverick alone. You might want to isolate him or her from the group so as not to affect others.

Impact on others

Will exceptions in your management of the some team members cause unrest with other telesales reps? Will they feel it is unfair?

Yes, in some cases, it will.

Here's what you do. Tell the offended reps that, once they hit 100 percent of objective all of the time, they too will have the exception applied to them. They'll have the flexibility granted to them because they will have earned it.

You're not being flippant here. The point is this: the standards you set are designed to make reps better at selling. If the rep isn't achieving his or her sales quota, help is clearly needed. That rep is in no position to complain.

Setting standards is not a punishment. Setting standards is the first step in implementing a highly successful strategy.

The new kid in town (the experienced rookie)

The new kid in town is the hotshot rookie of your organization. This is the experienced rep with noted sales success from another company or industry. What do you do?

A rookie to your organization is no different than a superstar athlete traded from one team to another. The star may have proven ability or skill, but the star must play within the team's playbook. Once the star has shown he can play within that context, there is room for individual genius and improvisation.

Train the new rep to your standards. Communicate to him or her that this is what is expected. Explain that your process works and that's why you have it. Once the rookie shows that he or she can sell within your standards, you can allow some flexibility.

Most experienced reps understand this and comply. If they are really as good as their reputation, they adapt, evolve, and succeed.

The inexperienced rookie

Inexperienced or unproven rookies? No question—they follow the standards you have set. Period. End of story. Until they show aptitude, ability, and success, they follow the team's game plan.

It's Not a Numbers Game—Setting Numeric Standards

"Telesales—it's a numbers game!"

How many times have you heard this?

In other words, "yes" lives in the land of "no," and if you dial long enough and hard enough, you'll get a sale. Pound the phone, so to speak.

There is absolutely no question that hard work is vital to success in telesales. And that's precisely why you have to be very, very careful when establishing numeric standards for dials, contacts, presentations, leads, sales, and whatever else you measure and calculate. It gets very easy for sales managers, executives, and owners to become so fixated on the attainment of numbers that they forget about the *results*.

Results versus numbers

The name of the game is results. If your sales reps achieve the sales objectives that you set, ease up as you would with a field sales rep. If a field sales rep is cranking 125 percent of objective, no manager will be flogging him or her to make three more visits per day. Never. Generally speaking, everyone is overjoyed at the success.

So why isn't this true in telesales?

Use your numbers as guidelines for directing focus and energy, not as an absolute measure. Concentrate on the results your reps are getting, and use the numbers to determine coaching rather than productivity requirements.

Setting numeric standards

Having said that, it is important to set some numeric standards. This gives your reps an indication of what is likely needed for good sales results. It gives them a goal, so they don't flounder, and it provides sound direction, so they don't get complacent.

There are four key numeric standards that should be addressed from a coaching perspective.

1. Sales results

Start your numeric standards by providing your reps with a clear revenue standard. This is the most important number because it is based on results. If you haven't already, break the objectives down from yearly, to quarterly, to monthly, to weekly, and to daily.

Depending on your company, your sales results might focus on revenue or on gross margin or on both—whatever works for you. The point is that this helps your telesales reps know precisely what they have to do.

2. Dials—a sliding standard

Who really knows how many dials it will take to achieve the sales results?

To establish an effective numeric standard, create a benchmark, or rule of thumb, for the number of dials that the reps will probably have to make. This number is based on your experience and knowledge of the market and your telesales application. Suppose, for example, it generally takes fifty dials to reach the optimum number of decision makers and generate the revenues necessary to achieve the objective.

If so, make fifty the sliding standard. A sliding standard means that if your rep hits his or her revenue objective at thirty-nine dials, he or she may not plough through another eleven dials. Cut that rep some slack because tomorrow will likely be different. He or she may have to make seventy-three dials to hit the numbers. You see my point? It all evens out in the wash. Don't forget this.

And if you focus on the results the reps need to achieve—rather than on achieving the activity numbers you set—you'll get top-notch sales.

3.   DMC—decision-maker contacts

Decision-maker contacts (DMCs) is the number of times your rep reaches and speaks to the person who makes the decision for that particular client. This is far more important than the number of dials because reaching a decision maker means an opportunity to sell.

The number of DMCs varies with product, industry, and sales type. Reaching purchasing agents is far easier than reaching surgeons. Reaching middle-level managers is a heck of a lot easier than CEOs. But usually, this can be determined by past experiences, and again, this should be used as a sliding scale gauge. However, for most B2B selling applications, a good rule of thumb for a DMC contact rate is about twenty to thirty per day.

Monitor the DMC rate closely because it is critical. If you have a goal of twenty-five DMCs and you have a rep who is averaging eighteen contacts, you should begin monitoring calls immediately. There could be any number of issues, such as too much pre-call planning or post-call wrap-up. It could suggest your rep is not effective at getting past gatekeepers. Or, it might suggest the rep is having lengthier conversations. This could be positive, but if the lengthy calls are not translating to sales, coaching is probably necessary.

4.   Phone time (talk time)

Talk time—the time spent connected with the decision maker—is an important standard that should be monitored on a regular basis. In most B2B scenarios with relatively simple transactions, the average talk time tends to range from two to three minutes. Your average talk time will vary depending on the complexity of the sale and whether you are calling prospects, existing clients, or both.

When monitoring talk time, look for anomalies. For instance, if the average talk time is 2.75 minutes and you have a rep consistently averaging 1.5 minutes, there is a good chance that corners are being cut. This is your clue to monitor the calls and assess the skill and quality level. In short, analyze what you hear and provide feedback accordingly.

Don't be misled by long talk time either. There is a popular belief that the longer the call, the more consultative and thorough the rep is. If your average call length is 2.75 minutes and your rep is averaging 6.50 minutes per call, that is your cue to monitor a series of calls. The rep may be doing a superb job, or the rep maybe rambling on at the cost of productivity and sales. Or it might be something in between. Check it out.

Of course, in every case, evaluate all the indicators against the rep's sales results. If a rep is fast on the phone (relative to talk time) and is 185 percent over his or her sales objective, you might not want to change a thing. Naturally, you should monitor calls to ensure quality and integrity, but assuming they are not an issue, let the rep be. If a rep takes three or four times longer per call and has a sale rate well below his or her objective, monitor, analyze, and provide feedback.

Remember that you can set standards for just about any activity. For instance, you might want to consider establishing a standard for e-mailing. But do not get too rigid on numeric standards. There are so many variables that impact the net result. Your average talk time might be 2.75 minutes, but if a rep is at 2.3 minutes or 3.4 minutes, use your common sense.

CHAPTER THREE

Step #2: Monitoring the Calls

The second step in the coaching process is monitoring the calls. This simply means taking the time to listen to the calls.

In this chapter:

- Monitoring—Revisited and Defined
- 2 Simple Ways to Monitor Calls
- 5 Methods of Monitoring
- Who Should Monitor Calls?
- When Should Calls Be Monitored?
- How Much Time Should You Spend Monitoring?
- Where Should You Conduct Monitoring?
- The 3 Times You Should Monitor
- What Should You Monitor?
- How You Should Monitor: The Yellow Sheet
- How to Build Your Own Monitoring Yellow Sheet
- Issues in Monitoring: Should You Advise Your Reps That You Will Be Monitoring Calls?
- The Monitoring Consent Form
- 7 Easy Steps for Dealing with Monitoring Paranoia

Monitoring—Revisited and Defined

There's nothing too complex about monitoring.

Monitoring is the process of listening to and observing a telesales rep's level of selling relative to a given standard.

The reason why we monitor is obvious: you can't provide feedback if you have not observed the call behavior. And while this is obvious, how you approach the monitoring process can impact its overall success.

2 Simple Ways to Monitor Calls

You can monitor calls in two ways: real-time calls and recorded calls. There are pros and cons to each.

Real-time calls

Monitoring a real-time call refers to listening to live calls as they occur. You can listen to a call as you sit next to the rep or from a remote location by keying in a special code. Either way, what you hear will be live.

The benefit of a real-time call is that you get an instant feel for what is happening on the floor with your reps. You can immediately begin to gauge the quality of the selling effort. What this really means is that you can provide real-time feedback, which helps modify the telesales rep's behavior right away.

On the other hand, live monitoring can be time-consuming and sometimes unproductive. For instance, you may spend an hour monitoring calls but never hear a live call. For whatever reason, the rep may have been unlucky and encountered voice mail instead of live decision-makers. No one is to blame, but the hour is likely to have been a poor use of time.

Recorded calls

You can also monitor recorded calls. Digital recording units can record every single call made (or taken) by your reps and sort them by rep, extension, time of day, length of call, date, or whatever; you name it. It's one of the most powerful technological tools you can purchase.

If you don't have digital recording, build a case study for why you should buy one. Here are four reasons why it makes sense to invest in one.

### 1.	Recordings make you more effective and save you hours of time.

Because digital recorders let you sort calls by any number of variables, you can zero in on calls that allow you to effectively assess the rep. For instance, sorting by call length allows you to quickly identify and disregard no-answer or voice mail calls. Longer length calls usually indicate a complete call. Of course, what this really does is make your monitoring time more effective and productive. You can skip minor calls and save time focusing only on calls that offer substance.

### 2.	Recordings give you flexibility.

Days get hectic. Problems arise. You firefight. Big meetings. Suddenly the day is over, but the monitoring hasn't been done. Digital recording also means you can access the recorder at any time of day or night. If your day gets a little too chaotic, you can still monitor a handful of calls later that night or early in the morning. I have even known managers to download calls to a CD or a Smartphone and listen to those calls on the commute to and from work.

3.   Recordings tell the truth.

But perhaps most significantly, digital recording allows the telesales rep to self-monitor his or her calls. This is a powerful way to coach. As you coach, you'll discover that some of your reps will live in denial. In other words, they will deny having said certain things or omitting others. It's human nature. When they hear themselves on tape, they are often awestruck. But once confronted with the issue, they are more open and receptive to the feedback.

4.   Recording can make training more effective.

When you hear a great call, whether in whole or in part, save it. Make it part of your training program, so new reps can hear exactly what a good call sounds like. If you hear a call that illustrates a typical example, save that call and use it in your training. Nothing communicates a message better than a real example.

Cautions

As much as I love digital recording, there are three important cautionary points. First of all, digital recording can sometimes be expensive. Much depends on your telephone system. I had a client who recently installed digital recording for less than five thousand dollars, but others have paid more.

Secondly, digital recording is not live, which means that by the time the call is monitored, the event might be hours or even days old. By the time you and your rep listen to the call, the feedback may not be as relevant. What's more, the change in the rep's behavior will not be instant, which means the substandard technique or skill will have been prolonged.

Finally, stemming from the second point, it gets very easy for a manager to put off monitoring because he or she knows the calls are being recorded. Suddenly the manager wakes up one morning to find that he or she has not monitored in ten days.

Overall, however, digital recording will make coaching easier, faster, more effective, more productive, and more successful. Check it out.

5 Methods of Monitoring

There are five ways or methods of listening in on a call.

1.   Eavesdrop

One of the most common ways to monitor a call is simply to eavesdrop. You might be seated with your rep or at your desk or simply walking around, and you catch a snippet of the call. Eavesdropping has an instantaneous quality to it. You heard something and you can provide feedback in the blink of an eye. It tells your reps that you keep an ear on the quality and effectiveness of their calls.

But the eavesdrop approach implies one-way monitoring, which means you hear your rep's side of the call, but you don't hear the client's side of the call. For that reason alone, eavesdropping is somewhat limited in terms of effectiveness. Without the client's conversation, it is hard to evaluate the rep's approach. Attempts to provide feedback can be met with resistance because the reps thinks, *yeah—but you didn't hear what the prospect said, so your feedback doesn't apply.* In fact, you can do a lot of damage to the coaching process if you are seen as petty, unfair, and inaccurate. Forewarned is forearmed.

Certainly there is a place for eavesdropping. If your opening statement has been scripted as a standard, you don't need to hear the customer's side of the conversation. Either the rep delivers the opening statement to-standard or not. You can also evaluate the tone, rate, and volume of your rep's voice based on this one-sided approach to monitoring. So use eavesdropping, but use it wisely.

2. Y-jack

The way to avoid the eavesdropping dilemma is with a Y-jack. The Y-jack is a device that plugs into your rep's telephone set and allows you to silently monitor your rep and the customer or the prospect. In this manner, you get both sides of the conversation. *Et voila*, problem solved.

Y-jacks are simple to use and inexpensive to purchase. They can be used by you to coach, and they can be used by your reps to monitor each other's calls. In particular, rookies can benefit from this type of monitoring.

3. Wireless handset

Depending on your phone system, you can monitor from a wireless handset. In effect, a code is entered with an extension number, and you can listen to the rep's call. You can do this seated right beside the rep, from another workstation, or from your office or the parking lot, if you like.

Wireless handsets work well if your physical presence right beside the rep in the cubicle is too intimidating and is impacting the rep's sales behavior. Often moving away five or ten feet gives reps a sense of space and comfort even if they know you are monitoring.

Wireless handsets are also great if a rep needs help with a call. For instance, I have a client in Tampa whose reps will raise their hands if confronted with a challenging call. The manager can zip on over, enter the code, and monitor the call. Depending on the circumstances, the manager can coach the rep with ideas and suggestions or take over the call if required.

4.   Monitoring Station

A monitoring station is a phone at a location other than the telesales rep's desk that allows you to enter a code and silently monitor any call. It's fast and easy to use.

The debate rages as to whether a tone should inform the telesales reps that they are being monitored. To this, I offer, *are you crazy?* A tone? Of course you should not have a tone. Right off the bat, a tone is distracting, buzzing away in their ears as they talk with clients. Secondly, it's disturbing to the reps who suddenly realize the calls are being monitored. Their behavior often changes only because they are aware of someone barging in. Don't use a tone.

5.   Monitoring by walking around (MBWA)

Monitoring by walking around is self-explanatory. It means casually walking around the cubicles or desks and listening in. While MBWA does not give you the same level of detail as the other methods suggested above, it does give you a feel for what is going on; it gives you sound bites. You can hear if the reps are on the phone, and at any given time you can assess if the reps are selling to the standards that have been set.

But here's the interesting thing about MBWA: your mere presence is often enough to ensure a degree of compliance relative to the standards. The more your reps comply, the more familiar they become with techniques and skills learned in training. This ultimately creates competency and, eventually, mastery. Their behaviors have now been changed.

Who Should Monitor Calls?

There is a hidden answer to this rather simple question, so bear with me for a moment. Who should monitor calls? Well, the manager or coach is the most obvious candidate. These individuals need to monitor to determine if the standards are being met and to provide appropriate feedback.

The fact of the matter is, anyone can monitor calls. Rookies, veterans, executives, owners, accountants, customer-service reps—anyone can monitor a call for whatever reason.

But—and here's the hidden part—*not everyone can provide feedback*. In fact, very few people can. More on this in the feedback section, but for now, know this: the only person who can provide feedback is the person who a) heard the call and b) is trained to provide feedback.

Nothing will destroy your coaching program faster than all sorts of unqualified people providing feeble advice. Remember that!

Who Should Be Monitored?

Should all reps be monitored on an equal and consistent basis?

No. Absolutely not!

Some reps will need more monitoring. Others should be monitored only on odd occasions. Others shouldn't be monitored at all. And the sooner you can come to grips with the inequities of the situation, the easier job will be.

The "A," "B," "C," and "R" of monitoring

Monitoring takes time, and time for most managers is a precious commodity. It is vital that you use the time wisely and strategically. By doing so, you will maximize your efforts and succeed at improving sales.

The way to accomplish this is to analyze your sales team based on its sales activity over several months. If you are like most sales teams, you can easily divide your sales reps into four simple categories. The categorization of each rep determines your approach to monitoring.

"A" reps

"A" reps are those reps who consistently meet and exceed their numbers. They are your breadwinners. You bank on them. These reps need minimal monitoring (and hence, minimal analysis and feedback) because they are achieving their goals.

This is not to say you shouldn't monitor their calls. Every now and then, sit with them or listen to their recorded calls to ensure they are not drifting. It also sends a message to your entire team that coaching is important for everyone. But the amount of time spent with this group should be minimal because you have other fish to fry. You want others on your team to move up the chain and join the "A" team.

"B" reps

"B" reps are those reps who sometimes meet their goals, and at other times, they fall short. They are somewhat inconsistent but fairly reliable in terms of doing their jobs. It is these reps who you want to spend as much time monitoring as you can. Why? Because they are on the cusp of becoming "A" reps. They have the potential. Usually, "B" players need a little kick in the butt or they need to learn how to finesse certain situations. Because of this, they are good candidates for the coaching process.

But here's the thing: by spending time with them, the return on your time investment will be significantly greater because the dollar volumes are bigger. At the end of the day, the goal is to improve sales and revenues. You get measured on that goal. So it makes sense to spend the time with those who are probably going to make it happen for you.

"C" reps

This leads us to "C" reps. "C" reps are those reps who are consistent underachievers. They may still be profitable for you, but they almost never meet their revenue goals.

Don't spend much time with them.

Let me repeat that: don't spend much time with them. This comment usually generates a good debate during my coaching workshops. The argument is that it is the manager's job to help these individuals reach the top. That's a noble goal, but any manager who's been around the block a couple of times knows that "C" reps almost inevitably stay "C" reps. It doesn't matter how much time and effort you spend with them, the "C" players seem genetically wired to stay mediocre.

This is not meant as a disparaging comment. "C" players can be good, kind, and wonderful people, but they are not gifted in terms of selling. When I coached hockey, I had lots of kids who had big hearts but limited talent. Coaching would only take them so far, and that was it.

One more thing—avoid the projects. The projects are those reps in your department who you think have all the potential in the world if only someone (you) would spend time with them. You know who I am talking about; these reps have the skill and show flashes of brilliance; they're just a heartbeat away from bursting the sales doors wide open if only someone (you) would give them a chance. And so we take an inordinate amount of time coaching the project because we can feel that he or she is almost there.

But they rarely seem to do it. And so you are left discouraged. But more significantly you realize the opportunity cost. You recognize that you could have spent time with others who would have taken to the coaching and succeeded.

Like "A" players, monitor your "C" players every now and then, but recognize that this is not the group that's going to take you to the promised land of sales.

The one exception might be if you have a rookie who is moving through the ranks of your company and is a "C" player, spend time with him or her. See "R" reps below.

"R" reps

An "R" rep is a rookie. This is someone you have recently hired and trained. Here is where you spend a ton of time monitoring.

The reason is obvious. Rookies are like a big white canvas. You want to paint your standards onto that canvas so that the skills are bold and brassy. You want the rookies to follow the standards you set so that they become successful faster. You don't want them to pick up bad habits or stray from the standards that were taught in training. If you do, it takes two or three times the effort to break bad habits compared to supporting good habits.

So, like your "B" reps, monitor your "R" reps thoroughly and completely. At some point, the rookie will find his or her way into the other categories. At that moment you can determine how much more or how much less time you'll spend with him or her.

Heartless and cynical?

Do I sound a bit heartless and cynical in the approach to monitoring? It is not meant that way. When you boil it down, your job is to produce a winning team that produces sales results. This means you must make some hard and fast decisions. Where you spend your time will dictate the ultimate outcome of your efforts.

So think long and hard about what I have just said.

How Much Time Should You Spend Monitoring?

How much time should you spend monitoring?

How long is a piece of string?

There is no clear answer. If your sales are dismal, you need to spend a heck of a lot more time in the trenches, monitoring and coaching than if your sales are tip-top.

Having said that, here are some rules of thumb.

The 50% rule

If you have just introduced a coaching program to your sales department, you can expect to spend as much as 50% of your day monitoring (which also includes analyzing and feedback).

Yep. You read that correctly—50%! You may need to kick-start the program to get your reps on board quickly. Of course, that doesn't mean you'll spend the rest of your management career monitoring. This is only temporary.

The 20% imperative

Once you have established your coaching program, or if your results are relatively decent, the rule of thumb for daily monitoring is 20%. This means about one and a half hours per day should be spent in the monitoring mode (which, again, includes time for analyzing and feedback).

It is best to do it in one chunk of time, maybe two. No more than that. You want to have continuity and flow in your monitoring. Five minutes here and ten minutes there won't cut it. Don't waste your time.

Commit to it now.

If you cannot find one and a half hours a day to help your reps improve and make the revenues you have been assigned as an objective, then don't bother implementing a coaching program.

It would be a sheer and utter waste of effort. It's kind of like an exercise program. Don't let anyone kid you; ten minutes of exercise might be nice, but it won't do a thing for your weight and fitness. The same is true with coaching.

Where Should You Conduct Monitoring?

Precisely *where* you conduct your monitoring activity can impact the sales behavior of your telephone sales team. By seeing you actively monitor their calls, they will tend to adhere more to the standards that have been set. Conversely, not seeing you can impact their behavior as well; some reps will ease off and take the path of least resistance.

There are three areas from where you can monitor calls: the rep's workstation, your workstation, and a remote location. Each has advantages and disadvantages.

1.   The telesales rep's workstation

Monitoring from your rep's workstation means sitting beside the rep and listening to calls using either a remote handset, a Y-jack, or simply hearing one side of the conversation.

The primary benefit is that you can *observe* the reps as well as monitor the call. You can literally *see* how the reps interact with the computer, if and how they take notes, how they access binders, job aids, and so forth. These behaviors can impact selling performance. A rep who is disorganized and searching for information on his or her desk or computer screen is probably not as focused on the customer or prospect. This dilutes the quality of the sell. Your subsequent feedback may be less about sales skills and more about organization.

Sitting beside the reps can also improve their sales "game." You'll find that many of your telephone reps will try a little harder and cut fewer corners. Simply by doing the activities because you're beside them will help them master the skills or techniques. Consequently, they will be more apt to continue using the skills after you move on.

Monitoring beside your reps also has the ripple effect of influencing the behavior of the adjacent reps. Everyone tends to up his or her sales game because the boss is there.

Similarly, you can multitask and monitor the calls of those around you. You can do this in between live calls with your rep.

Finally, when it comes time to providing feedback, you will be right there. The rep does not have to leave the workstation. This saves you and your rep time and effort.

On the other hand, there are two major disadvantages of monitoring beside your reps in their workstations. The first is that it can make them self-conscious and impact their sales behavior. It can be disruptive. While some reps will perform better, some will not simply because they are nervous. They stutter or forget or screw up, not because they don't know the skill, but because of your looming presence. In other words, you might end up coaching a behavior that is not really typical. While most get used to you at some point, others may not, and you might want to monitor from another location.

The second disadvantage of monitoring beside your rep is that it can be time-consuming and not always productive. You could literally sit for an hour and not hear a completed call because the rep was unable to reach decision makers.

In addition, plunking yourself in the middle of the calling floor invites interruption. Other reps can and will drop by with a question or two. It can quickly become disruptive and annoying for both you and the rep you are monitoring.

2. Your workstation or office

You can—and sometimes should—monitor from your office or workstation.

When you're at your desk, you can multitask between calls, which makes you a little more productive in your time-starved day. On the other hand, be aware of the fact that other tasks and action items will constantly tempt you. It gets easy to forget about the monitoring.

Depending on the monitoring capabilities of your phone and computer system, you might be able to monitor numerous calls simultaneously. When one of your telephone reps connects, you can quickly log in and monitor that call. This improves productivity.

Monitoring from your desk also improves the odds that you'll hear a more natural presentation from your rep. Rather than presenting an A game or being nervous because you're sitting there, he or she is more likely to use a typical skill set. (Note: keep in mind that it doesn't take long for your telephone team to figure out you're monitoring calls.)

3. A remote location

A remote location refers to a private office that's separated from the telephone calling area.

There are two reasons why you might want to remotely monitor calls. First, it virtually eliminates interruptions from your reps and others. This means you can concentrate on the coaching process and stay focused. It also reduces or eliminates multitasking that occurs when you sit at your desk.

Second, you'll hear your reps in their most natural states. It's a superb way to determine if the "mice will play when the cat's away." I hope your reps intuitively understand that following the selling standards will make them more successful and that cutting corners or diluting their skills doesn't pay off. But the fact of the matter is some reps will lapse. It pays to find out and coach accordingly.

This leads to the one major disadvantage of monitoring from a remote location. Your reps might get the impression that you are spying on them. It's an understandable result, but don't let this perception stop you from using this approach from time to time. It is vital to your success, to your company's success, and to your reps' success. You need to gauge sales behavior. Ultimately, you are trying to help your telesales reps be more successful in selling. If they *choose* to pare down their selling effort while you're away, the issue is *their* behavior, not yours.

So, which monitoring system should you use? Use all three. Don't get stuck using one because you'll miss out on the benefits of the others. Make a conscious decision to shake up your monitoring location. You'll be fascinated by what you discover. But, at the end of day, your reps will discover that, for their own sakes, it is best to adhere to quality and consistency.

The 3 Times You Should Monitor

1. Every day

Monitor every single day. Make a habit of it. Remember that the coaching process is an "important, but not urgent" task. It gets very,

very easy to put it aside with the promise that you'll get to it later. Later becomes even later, and you know how that routine goes.

Monitoring everyday also puts you right in the thick of things. You will know what's happening on the floor. You can gauge things immediately.

Monitoring every day also tells your telesales team that the coaching process is serious business. This will encourage the reps to apply the standards that you have set on a more consistent basis. Remember homeostasis? Homeostasis is the tendency for individuals to lapse back into old behaviors. If you are there monitoring on a daily basis, homeostasis become less of an issue.

2.   At scheduled times

Schedule your monitoring. If you sit down with your Outlook, your planner, or whatever you use to plan your day, block out time for monitoring. This is a classic time management technique that has a high degree of success. When you make an appointment to monitor, and it is visible to the eye, it is more likely to be done.

Scheduling has another couple of benefits. If others have access to your calendar and are requesting a meeting, they'll see that you have time allotted for monitoring and that time cannot be scheduled for an appointment. If you don't have it blocked, you can bet someone will snatch the time away from you.

Speaking of which, scheduling is a great way to fend off your boss. When he wants to see you or schedule a meeting at a conflicting time, you simply say, "I can't make it at two o'clock. I have a meeting scheduled with my sales team. How about 3:30?" This little trick doesn't always work but it can work from time to time. If your boss is serious about achieving revenue objectives, he or she will respect your monitoring appointment.

3. Varied times

Let me tell you a true story about human behavior and sales results.

A while ago, we introduced a coaching program into a company. The five managers were not keen about it. They claimed it took too much time and there were too many interruptions; it was the whole gamut of lame excuses. The VP of sales took action. He mandated that all five managers monitor from 2:00-3:30 every day from a remote location on another floor.

Guess what happened? On a subsequent visit a month later, I reviewed the sales reports and activity logs and noticed a spike in sales results. Every day from 2:00 to about 3:30, sales were up by 31 percent compared to any other time of the day.

It took me a while to put the two events (monitoring and results) together, but we all found it rather interesting. It screamed that when reps knew the coaching process was being implemented, they worked at implementing the standards. Because they implemented the standards, sales were up during that part of the day.

Here's another interesting note. After 3:30, sales were almost nonexistent. The reps knew they weren't being monitored, so they slacked off.

One could write volumes about the implications of this little test, but the solution for the company was to have the managers monitor at various times through the day. Usually they monitored alone or in pairs, but never as a group. We implemented monitoring at desks as well as from remote locations. The net results were fewer spikes and more sales throughout the day.

What Should You Monitor?

Skills

Obviously, monitor the standards that you have set for the skill sets. The whole purpose of creating standards is so that you have some objective measurements.

Product Knowledge

But you do not have to limit monitoring to skills. You could monitor product knowledge and determine if the telesales rep needs additional training or coaching feedback. But be aware that setting a standard for product knowledge can be challenging; knowledge of products or services is not typically process related. In the case of knowledge, if the rep makes a mistake or does not clearly know the product, treat it with feedback designed to reinforce the knowledge.

Computers, data, and customer relationship management (CRM)

Similarly, you can monitor reps relative to their ability to interact and use the computer, the database, and the CRM system. Like knowledge, setting standards for knowledge of databases or CRMs is challenging and unlikely to be worth the time. Reps learn this on the job. Your monitoring is designed to assess where they are in the learning process and provide feedback to expedite that learning, correct mistakes, suggest ways to improve, etc.

Delivery

Because telesales is an audio-based medium, monitor the delivery of the presentation by the rep. In other words, how the rep sounds is as important as what he or she says. There are three categories that you can monitor.

1.   Pace

Pace refers to the speed at which the rep recites the opening, the questioning, the presentation etc. If the rep is too quick in his or her delivery, the client can consciously or subconsciously visualize someone who is trying to pull a fast one. In other words, the quicker the delivery, the more likely it will create distrust in the client's mind. Similarly, too slow a delivery can conjure an image of a rep who is disinterested or uncertain. Either way, it is a no-win situation.

2.   Volume

If a rep tends to be loud, the client often perceives him or her as overbearing and aggressive. This may not be accurate or fair, but perception is reality in the client's mind. If the volume is too low, one gets the feeling that the rep lacks confidence and is difficult to hear.

3.   Tone

Tone is the emotional quality of words. It's how we say things and how they are conveyed. For instance, a monotone voice suggests the rep is reading a script. If a rep is presenting a new and exciting development in the latest software upgrade, his or her tone should suggest excitement. Sarcasm sometimes creeps into the delivery, especially if a rep has had a bad streak in selling and is discouraged or annoyed. Speaking of annoyance, clients can quickly glean that a rep has had a bad day; they can sense that the call is an onerous task.

Warning!

Monitoring delivery does not come without some challenges. It is difficult to standardize delivery.

Take pace for example. Most of us speak at a rate of 140 to 160 words per minute. We process those words about three times as fast as we hear them. The point is, how do you measure and assess if the pace was say, 135 or words or 171 words per minute? It's a gut feeling kind of thing. Gut feelings can be a disaster when providing feedback. What *you* consider too fast might be normal for the rep. The same applies to volume and tone. They are both interpretative.

There is no clear rule of thumb other than common sense. If the rep is virtually booming away, you can provide feedback to lower it a bit. If the tone is dull and dreary and consistently so, you can bring this to the rep's attention. But the key point is that it has to be obvious. There are shades of gray in the interpretation.

Monitor delivery, but monitor wisely and carefully.

How You Should Monitor: The Yellow Sheet

Monitoring calls can be challenging, especially if you have created a variety of standards for various skills sets. How do you monitor fairly, accurately, and consistently?

The answer is simple: develop a monitoring sheet.

A monitoring sheet is a job aid that lists the key elements of your standards for all parts of the call. In effect, it acts like a checklist to remind you of the standards that have been set. When you listen to calls, live or taped, have that sheet in front of you as a prompt. If the monitoring sheet lists five components for the opening statement, then listen to ensure that these components have been implemented. Easy as pie.

Is a monitoring sheet a thinly disguised report card?

No.

But mention a monitoring sheet and in no time flat, you'll hear someone suggest that it is a report card. (Who liked report cards when they were kids?) Or mention a monitoring sheet and you'll often find someone who wants to grade and weight the call components so that a score can be obtained.

The purpose of the monitoring sheet is simply to determine if the reps are using the skill sets that you defined in training. Are they using the standard operating procedures or not? The monitoring sheet is not a grading sheet. Assigning weight and creating a score is a subjective and destructive waste of time.

You want to use the monitoring sheet only as a tool in the coaching process. This means that when it is time to give feedback to the rep, you have something objective to refer to. That's it. It is meant to help you help the reps.

How to Build Your Own Yellow Monitoring Sheet

Creating a monitoring sheet is relatively easy. The trick is to keep it simple. Remember your objective is to ensure that your reps are implementing the selling standards that you established in your training program. The sheet helps you determine if they are doing just that.

Step #1:   Identify your key standards.

The first step is to identify the standards. Throughout the book, I have alluded to several standards. For most clients, here is a broad list of selling standards:

- Pre-call planning
- Opening statements for prospects
- Opening statements for follow-up calls to prospects
- Opening statements for existing clients
- Managing gatekeepers
- Dealing with initial objections from clients
- Questioning and qualifying
- Presenting an offer
- Closing or advancing a sale
- Dealing with objections, questions, and concerns

Step #2:   Define the standard in detail.

This step adds detail to the standard. It identifies precisely what you expect from the rep for that particular standard. You can be very specific or you can be broader based. A good example that illustrates this point is the opening statement. For example, here is a 5-step process that I have mentioned in the early chapters that could be used on the monitoring sheet:

Opening statement	To-standard	Not to-standard
• Full name	☐	☐
• Company name	☐	☐
• Reason for call	☐	☐
• Benefit to prospect	☐	☐
• Bridge to a question	☐	☐

In this example, the telesales reps have a degree of latitude in what they say. As long as they follow the five components in the opening statement, the call is considered to-standard. This allows a degree of flexibility in the approach made by the reps and helps reduce the canned nature that some calls can have. It works particularly well with more veteran telephone reps who have experience and knowledge.

On the other hand, some clients prefer a much more scripted approach to opening statements.

> Dr._____. My name is_____, and I am calling from _____.
> Dr._____, we are expanding our network of physicians, and your name came
> up as a possible candidate. I am not sure if our program would be of benefit
> to your practice, but if I have caught you at a good time, I would like to ask
> you a few quick questions.

☐ To-standard ☐ Not to-standard

To-standard   Not to-standard

In this real-life example, the standard for the opener is scripted word-for-word. It is given to rookie reps because it works better than any other approach tested. The rep does *not* have a choice and is not allowed to vary it.

It is similar with questioning; some companies list the types of questions that the rep should ask when qualifying. For example,

Qualifiers	To-standard	Not to-standard
• Needs questions	☐	☐
• Budget questions	☐	☐
• Time-frame questions	☐	☐
• Decision-maker questions	☐	☐

Like the opening statement, this portion of the monitoring sheet offers greater flexibility and creativity. The *way* the rep identifies a need or asks about budget availability can vary from rep to rep and situation to situation. So long as it is *asked*, the rep can use any means at his or her disposal.

Again, with a savvier group of reps, this type of approach to monitoring (and to the entire coaching process) can be very effective because it ensures call quality without getting too microscopic.

On the other hand, the reps in the medical example cited above have three specific questions (qualifiers) that *must* be asked:

Qualifying questions	To-standard	Not to-standard
• What type of insurances do you take?	☐	☐
• Are you seeing new patients?	☐	☐
• What types of therapies do you practice?	☐	☐

This particular client has standardized these questions because they are vital to determining if a doctor qualifies for the program or not.

But more significantly, the client knows that the attention span of a doctor is limited and that it is *vital* that the rep get to the heart of the questioning right away; otherwise, the doctor will terminate. So there is no quibbling. The rep is expected to qualify to-standard.

Step #3:   Avoid ratings scales.

There is a strong tendency for some managers to score the calls; rate them on a scale of one to three or one to five. Here is a simple example of what I mean:

	Poor	Weak	Okay	Good	Great
Opening	1	2	(3)	4	5
Questioning	1	2	3	(4)	5
Presentation	1	(2)	3	4	5

Look familiar?

The spirit behind the scale seems benign enough. It is designed to assess the gap in the performance of scale. If the rep knocks off a "5," there is no gap, and everyone is pleased as punch. If the rep manages a "1," there is trouble in paradise. Obviously work needs to be done.

All of that is fine in theory, but in reality, it is another story. For the most part, managers will lump the majority of their evaluations into the "3" category. It is the easiest thing to do when evaluating a rep, and it reduces rep defensiveness.

Additional challenges occur when a call is rated, say, at a "2" or a "4." Suppose your rep asks, "Well, how do I get to a "3" or a "5?" You'd better have a specific step-by-step process to get to the next level. If you don't, you've exposed the weakness of the scale. The weakness is the subjectivity, and that means your feedback has no basis in sound fact—only in your opinion. It won't hold water.

So don't waste your time with silly scales. (We'll revisit rating scales again when we talk about feedback.)

Step #4: Use a binary scale.

There is only one scale you should employ for your monitoring sheet—a binary scale.

It's not much of a scale. Binary means two. You only have two choices to make when you monitor a standard. These choices are to-standard or not to-standard. If you look at the examples above, the scale is binary.

Think of how powerful this diminutive little scale really is. First, it evaluates whether the rep performed to the standard you set or not. There are no shades of gray. Second, it clearly forces you to make the call. There is no uncertainty. There is no "3" escape clause. You can't run; you can't hide. And neither can the rep. If the standard is important to the success of the call, there is no debate.

Step #5: Leave room for comments.

Your sheet should have room for a few words. You might use it to reference the particular client or to note something specific about the call or to provide your approach to feedback.

Step #6:   Use one sheet of paper.

This is a simple tip, but use one sheet of paper. If need be, use both sides. Why? It's less cumbersome.

Step #7:   Copy it on yellow paper.

Here's a nifty coaching tip. Copy your monitoring sheet on brightly colored paper. I use yellow because, when I haul it out, everyone can see I am monitoring.

Guess what tends to happen? Your reps begin to comply with the standard. They become a little more careful and diligent. As they use the standard more they become more competent and confident with it. Better.

But here's an added bonus. If you are monitoring by walking around (MBWA), use a clipboard with a stack of yellow paper. As mentioned, the reps start to comply. In the meantime, you can actually be working on other tasks such as reading reports or working on projects. The reps don't realize this, of course, but they will put in the effort. Hence, you get more done!

(Note: do not do this all the time. You do want to monitor, but there are times when it is more convenient to proverbially kill two birds with one stone.)

Sample monitoring sheet

Here is a real-life example of a monitoring sheet.

Monitoring Sheet Example

Inside Rep _____ Date _____ Monitored by _____

Planning & Preparation	S	NS	Notes
❑ completes green sheet to plan calls	☐	☐	
❑ uses green sheet during call	☐	☐	

Opening Statements	S	NS	Notes
❑ Name	☐	☐	
❑ Company	☐	☐	
❑ Reason for Call	☐	☐	
❑ Benefit	☐	☐	
❑ Bridge to Question	☐	☐	

Possible Coaching Prompts (trigger phrases)
- o Mancini – "I am not sure…"
- o Sobczak – "Depending on your situation…"
- o Time – "If I've caught you at a good time…"
- o Other

Questioning	S	NS	N/A	Notes
❑ uses questions to establish rapport	☐	☐	☐	
❑ uses questions to identify possible needs	☐	☐	☐	
❑ uses question to gather additional info	☐	☐	☐	

Possible Coaching Prompts
- o open ended questions (Too many? Too little? Examples or suggestions?)
- o close ended questions (Too many? Too little? Examples or suggestions?)

Presentation (the "Pitch")	S	NS	N/A	Notes
❑ Offer – presents offer, solution. idea etc.	☐	☐	☐	
❑ Explanation – expands on offer; details	☐	☐	☐	
❑ Benefit – provides specific benefit	☐	☐	☐	
❑ Uses OEB chart – if applicable	☐	☐	☐	

Closing and/or Advance	S	NS	N/A	Notes
❑ Asks for sale or decision	☐	☐	☐	
❑ Uses silence to allow client to answer	☐	☐	☐	
❑ Advances sale (sets specific time & date)	☐	☐	☐	

Objections Handling	S	NS	N/A	Notes
❑ Knee Jerk (uses "Empathize. Ignore, Ask")	☐	☐	☐	
❑ Smokescreen (uses "Empathize, Clarify, Respond")	☐	☐	☐	
❑ Uses Job Aids (objections chart))	☐	☐	☐	

Wrap Up	S	NS	N/A	Notes
❑ adds notes to file	☐	☐	☐	
❑ sets follow up date	☐	☐	☐	

Issues in Monitoring: Should You Advise Your Reps That You Will Be Monitoring Calls?

Yes—and no.

Sometimes tell your reps when you'll be monitoring. (Of course, if you are crowded in beside them, they'll quickly figure it out!)

Sometimes don't tell you reps you'll be monitoring. Go to a remote location, and listen in.

If you have positioned coaching as a positive event, it won't matter whether you tell your reps if you are monitoring or not. They will see the benefits of coaching quickly enough, so your monitoring will not freak them out. In fact, they will welcome it.

But the important thing to understand is that coaching is about modifying behavior. Sometimes monitoring without advising your reps helps you determine if they are buying into the concept or if they lapse into old behaviors when you are absent from the floor.

Remember that change is difficult, and there is a natural tendency for reps to go back to old behaviors. You need to monitor that.

Is this spying?

It's only spying if you are trying to catch your reps lapsing into old behaviors, and if you provide a negative consequence for that lapse. If the rep doesn't sell to-standard, you treat it as if you were monitoring right beside the rep in his or her cubicle. You simply provide the feedback without lecture, sarcasm, or rebuke.

Eventually, your reps will recognize that lapsing to old behaviors isn't going to be tolerated and that you'll continuously urge them to modify. And consequently, they'll make the change for the better.

The Monitoring Consent Form

Sometimes it is wise to ensure that everyone knows, understands, and agrees to the monitoring of their calls, including recording. Every now and then, a situation arises where a telesales rep may claim that he or she was unaware of any monitoring. This is where a monitoring consent form comes in.

The form simply notifies the telesales rep, in writing, that calls can and will be monitored and recorded (if applicable). Moreover, the rep consents to it. In this manner, there is no miscommunication and no misunderstanding.

Monitoring And Taping Consent Form

I, _____, understand that from time to time my telephone calls will be monitored and/or taped for the express purpose of assessing call quality and to provide a means for effective, positive coaching feedback to help improve selling skills and techniques.

I further understand that my calls may be monitored and /or taped at any time and that I may or may not be notified ahead of time. This is done because of convenience and because of the need to provide effective coaching in a normal day to day work environment.

From time to time monitoring will be conducted at my work area so that coaching feedback can be provided on my calls, my computer skills, software knowledge and work habits.

I agree to the monitoring and/to taping of my calls for these purposes.

Signed this _____ day of _____ in the year of _____.

_____   _____
employee   manager

Notice how the form indicated that monitoring is used for "positively coaching and improving sales performance." This is the pact you are making with your reps. Tempting as it might be, do not use the monitoring of calls for negative purposes such as termination. If monitoring is used for censure or termination, your coaching program will be seen as a threat, and monitoring will be seen as negative.

Not all companies use monitoring consent forms. Only you can decide the benefits of the form. However, typically it is used when a new telesales rep is hired. It is signed, and a copy given to the rep. The original is saved in the rep's personnel file.

7 Easy Steps for Dealing with Monitoring Paranoia

A final word about the entire monitoring process: be aware that if calls haven't been monitored in the past, or if the monitoring has been rather transitory, you may encounter a degree of resistance from your reps.

Some of your reps may have come from companies where monitoring or quality control was used to grade the calls or used to find something wrong. Don't be surprised when you encounter this. There are numerous companies that have abused the coaching process and have used monitoring as a big stick. Be sensitive to that.

What to do?

There are seven simple steps to dealing with paranoia.

1.   Formally announce your coaching program.

Or, if you have an existing coaching program, announce that it is being revamped. Do this in a group setting.

2.   Position the coaching initiative as a positive event.

Make it a big event. Bring in pizza. Have music. Get the executives there. Tell them that presidents of companies have executive coaches. Heck, tell them that even top professional athletes have coaches. Explain the positives of the program and how it will help the reps to achieve success and improve sales. Talk about the training you provide and how you will ensure that the skills are used on a consistent basis. Tell them about homeostasis.

3.   Vow to your reps that coaching will not be used for censure.

Hit that negative nail right on the head. Acknowledge that, in the past, for some reps at different companies, coaching was used negatively, but that's not how it will be at your company.

4.   Describe the 4-step coaching process. Fully explain about standards, monitoring, analyzing, and feedback.

Show them the yellow monitoring sheet. Hide nothing. Explain that you'll monitor silently from afar sometimes and often right at their desks. No big deal.

5.   Deal with any questions or concerns right up front.

Ask for questions. Ask for feedback. Answer candidly.

6. **Let everyone know you'll be monitoring on the floor, at their stations, or at your desk.**

Do not use a remote location for the first couple of weeks. Keep them in the loop in the early stages. Once they discover it doesn't hurt one bit, they'll begin to accept it.

7. **Initially, celebrate and communicate victories and victories only**.

If Mark nails his opening statement as per standard, laud it. If Morgan overcomes an objection using the four-step process, stop the presses and share it. It doesn't matter if they got a sale, and it doesn't matter if the rest of their calls were mediocre or poor. In the early stages of your coaching program, publicly celebrate the victory. There'll be plenty of time to deal with constructive feedback. For now, you only want that warm, fuzzy feeling that monitoring—and subsequent feedback—doesn't hurt.

CHAPTER FOUR

Step #3: The Analyzing Process

This is a short chapter, and it focuses on the third step of the coaching process, which is analysis.

In this chapter:

- Analyzing—Revisited and Defined
- 4 Reasons Why You Should Take the Time to Analyze
- What to Analyze
- The Secret to Consistent and Accurate Analysis:
- The Algorithm Chart Explained
- What Else to Analyze—Call Results

While it may be a short chapter, analysis is a vital step. Without analysis, your feedback will inevitably become arbitrary and subjective. In no time flat, your telesales reps will pick up on the inconsistencies, and at some level, they will completely dismiss your feedback. The net result? No change in behavior. And no change in sales either.

Analyzing—Revisited and Defined

Analyzing is the third component in the coaching equation. Defined, **analyzing is the process of determining if the telesales rep is performing to the established standard and determining the action required based on the analysis.**

That's a fancy way of saying that analyzing is stopping to think about what you have just heard the rep say and determining if the skill or technique was performed to the standard, below the standard, or above the standard. Analyzing is also the process of determining what to do next. In other words, it also means formulating your approach to provide feedback to the rep.

That's it. Not hard. Analyzing is thinking about the call and about how you want to approach your feedback.

4 Reasons Why You Should Take the Time to Analyze

Once you begin the coaching process and you get some experience under your belt, you'll find that analyzing takes only a few seconds. But those few seconds can be the difference between effective, behavior-changing feedback and destructive, ineffective feedback. Here are some compelling reasons why you should invest those few seconds to analyze every single call.

1.   It prevents "foot in the mouth" disease.

The number one reason why you want to analyze the call before you provide feedback is to prevent putting your foot in your mouth. Period.

If you monitor a call and provide feedback too hastily, you run the risk of saying something that might not be accurate, appropriate, or effective. This will dilute and reduce the quality of your feedback.

But more significantly, it can impinge the entire coaching process. If your feedback is incomplete, inaccurate, harsh, subjective, unfair, confusing, petty, or useless, chances are you will lose the respect of the reps. Oh, they may nod their heads in agreement, but in their hearts and minds, they'll dismiss the feedback. When they do that, the behavior will not be modified, and you will have achieved nothing except a disgruntled sales rep.

2. It helps provide better feedback.

Apart from not sticking your foot in your mouth, analyzing helps determine the nature of your feedback. It gives you time to develop an approach to what you say and how you want to say it. Analyzing accounts for whether or not what you heard is an aberration or trend. It helps you determine if it is worth your time to provide feedback. In addition, you can assess where you want to provide the feedback—at the rep's desk, at your desk, or at a remote location. As noted earlier, these factors impact the quality of the feedback.

3. It permits customized feedback.

Similar to better feedback, customized feedback is feedback that is specific to that particular rep. Analysis helps you do that. Some reps may have a personality whereby a direct, "hit it on the head" approach works best. Other reps may have a personality where a subtle kid-gloved approach works better. Thinking about *who* is getting the feedback can determine *how* you want to provide the feedback.

4.   It positions you as a good coach.

Taking the time to analyze a call and provide better and more customized feedback makes you a better coach. Your reps will see you as fair and equitable. This makes them more and more receptive to more coaching. They will welcome it and you. Word gets around fast. Everything becomes that much easier.

What to Analyze

This might be the shortest section in the entire book.

> *Analyze the standards.*

Using your monitoring sheet, you analyze the standards that you have set.

Taking the time to identify and establish your standards is the key. In this manner, you are focusing on those aspects of the sales call that are important and significant to success. Analyze those items and nothing more.

The Secret to Consistent and Accurate Analysis

The absolutely amazing analysis algorithm

The secret to analyzing a call quickly, easily, consistently, and accurately is by using the absolutely amazing analysis algorithm job aid.

It's called absolutely amazing because it provides a process of logical thinking that you can apply to any call or portion of a call. By following the process, your analysis is guaranteed to be more accurate, which in turn impacts the quality of your feedback. And the better the feedback, the better the rep will be able to modify his or her behavior.

You'll quickly discover that the algorithm is simple to follow and even simpler to master. Not unlike "muscle memory" in sports, where enough repetition makes a skill an automatic response, the algorithm creates "mind memory" where enough repetition makes the process of thinking and analyzing an automatic response.

When to use the algorithm

- Use the algorithm when you first introduce your coaching program.
- Use it if you are a new manager of a telesales program and you don't know the backgrounds and histories of your telesales team.
- Use it if you have numerous telesales reps who require monitoring.
- Use it with rookies who may not have received all the necessary training.
- Use it when you are uncertain about a given situation—err on the side of caution.

The Analysis Algorithm

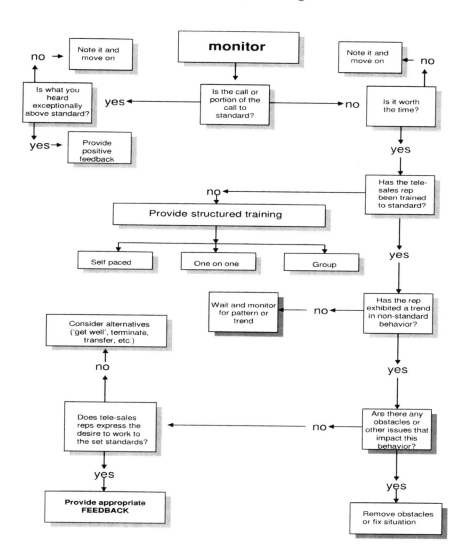

The Algorithm Chart Explained

The chart is self-explanatory, but here is the sum of its parts, taken apart and detailed for easy reference.

Monitor

The algorithm starts with the monitoring of a live or recorded call.

Is the call or portion of the call to-standard?

Based on what you have heard about the call or a portion of the call, ask yourself, "Is the skill or process to-standard?"

No quibbling here; if your standards have been clearly defined, the call or portion of the call is either to-standard or it is not.

Yes—to-standard

If the call is to-standard, note it and move on. But if the call, or a portion of the call, is exceptionally good, use it to provide positive feedback.

No—not to-standard—is it worth the time?

Okay, you monitored a call, and you noted a nonstandard issue. Ask yourself, "Is it worth my time?"

Maybe you have monitored a seasoned rep who's a top performer and who did not handle an objection to the precise standards you set. Perhaps you decide it is not worth your time at this stage because, with this rep, it's no big deal. On the other hand, you might consider it worth the time if a rookie rep or a "B" rep is struggling to obtain his or her numbers.

Has the rep been trained to-standard?

In most cases, the rep is on the floor, making sales calls, because he or she has been trained on the standards, so this question may not be applicable. But suppose the rep presents a new product solution to a client about which he or she has not received formal training.

In this case, coaching is not the appropriate strategy. Training is the route to go. Depending on the situation you can implement self-paced, one-on-one or group training. Coaching should be a short, quick process of reinforcement or reminding; it should not be used to give ten minutes of off-the-cuff training.

So, you must think!

Has the rep exhibited a trend in not to-standard behavior?

Here's a simple example. You've monitored five calls, and the rep has opened the calls using the five-step standard that you established in training. However, on the sixth call, the rep omits the benefit statement, an important part of a good, effective opening statement. What do you do?

Sure, you could provide legitimate, objective feedback, but was what you heard a trend or an aberration? If you do provide feedback at this moment, you run the risk of being perceived as a petty nag. Monitor a few more calls; see if the omission becomes a trend or if the rep simply forgot a portion of the opening on a single call.

This is a very important point; pay heed.

Are there any obstacles or other issues that impact this behavior?

Obstacles refer to anything that might have had an impact on the sales behavior. For instance, were there any distractions (noises, commotion, etc.) that impacted the concentration of the rep? Does the rep lack job aids such as an 'objections chart' that might improve the skill set? Perhaps a slow computer prevented the rep from accessing a product description, which in turn impacted his presentation.

If so, your feedback should be tempered by this fact.

Remove or fix the obstacle

Does the rep express a desire or willingness to work to-standard?

Here is an equally important question you must ask yourself. Has the rep shown himself or herself to be open to feedback? Remember the three kinds of reps from the beginning of the book—those who *can* be coached, those who *can't* be coached, and those who *won't* be coached.

Presumably the majority of your team is open to feedback, so provide it using the techniques provided in this book.

But if the rep repeatedly performs at substandard behavior (despite training, coaching, and encouragement) you can probably bet your feedback is going to fall on deaf ears. If so, coaching will be a waste of time, and you should consider other options, assuming the rep is not meeting sales objectives either.

The algorithm is simply a method of thinking. It helps remove some of the emotional elements that typically enter into the equation. This is not to say that emotion shouldn't play a part in your analysis. Sometimes there are circumstances that should be considered. But for the most part, this process provides a relatively fair and consistent methodology for analysis.

What Else to Analyze—Call Results

Of course, analysis is not simply limited to the standards you set. You can and should analyze individual call statistics and reports. You probably do this already, but a quick assessment of the number of dials, the number of decision-maker contacts, and the number of presentations, leads and sales will all help contribute to your analysis and subsequent feedback.

The single most important point to understand about call results is that they act as a bird dog. In other words, they point you in the right direction. By examining the call results, you will often get an indication of who might not be performing and might require coaching. What is more, the key indicators can help you develop a hypothesis so that you can direct your monitoring efforts.

Sales results

This is the most important statistic you should be measuring. It's all about the sales results. If the results are there, and if they are there consistently, then the rep is doing something right. Personally, I don't spend too much time with consistent "A" reps because there are plenty of others who need the quality coaching time. I don't care if that top rep is performing exactly to-standard, provided his or her approach is ethical and aboveboard. I don't fret if the dials and talk time are low. I am happy, delighted, overjoyed, elated, and satisfied.

If the sales results are *not* there, I dig into the other call results and activities. I look at dials and DMCs (decision maker contacts) and talk time to develop a possible hypothesis. And so should you.

Dials

Use dials only as an indicator of activity, not as an indicator of effectiveness. This is important, and I have been harping at it throughout the text. Sales are about results, not about dials. Use dials as a guideline to assess productivity issues, but not as an absolute measuring stick.

Again, if your rep is 117 percent to objective for the month and has made only 44 dials versus the required 50, give yourself and the rep a break. Cracking the whip and getting 16 more dials out of this rep is typically counterproductive. The rep will resent it, as well he or she should. Sure, the rep will probably burn through those extra dials, but with little or no regard for the net result.

On the other hand, if your rep is at 87 percent of objective and is only cranking out 44 dials per day, then you need to provide feedback regarding productivity.

Or you may want to monitor and observe the rep in question to determine if it is really a productivity issue or if it is an effectiveness issue. The rep may be engaging in long, ineffective conversations. Feedback might be required. It might be a planning issue or perhaps a questioning issue.

If the dial rate is extremely high, don't necessarily rejoice. A high dial rate may indicate that the rep is not effective at reaching the decision maker. Coaching feedback might be required relative to handling the gatekeeper. A high dial rate can burn out your rep and burn up your list. Don't squander either.

Use dials as one indicator. If a red flag goes up (i.e., the rep is below the slated numbers) do some analysis. Gauge the indicator against the results before you go storming in.

Decision-maker contacts (DMCs)

A DMC is an extremely important indicator to monitor and assess. It is defined as 'reaching and speaking to the person who can ultimately make the sale.' Reaching decision makers is more important than dials because decision makers mean sale opportunities. Look at DMCs daily because they can help point you in the right coaching direction.

For instance, suppose your rep has a high contact rate but a low sale rate. You can hypothesize that the rep is effective at getting to decision makers but might be ineffective at capturing their attention. Perhaps the opening statement has been diluted or maybe the questioning is incomplete. Who knows until you monitor, but at least you have a place to start.

Talk time

Some companies go absolutely nuts when it comes to talk time. To them, talk time is seen as the holy grail of telesales. The longer the call, the better. The more time reps spend in talk mode per hour the better.

However, talk time can be deceiving. Your call reports do not indicate if the talk time was time spent in conversation with a decision maker or time spent listening to an auto attendant or time spent listening to and leaving messages in voice mail. And the trouble is, if you push the talk time too hard, your reps will find a way to achieve the talk-time goal. Unfortunately, some (maybe many) will seek non-productive ways to make their talk-time objectives.

Of course, talk time is important, but how can you really assess it? This is why focusing on results makes much more sense. If the reps are achieving their sales objectives based on 1.5 minutes per call, then glory halleluiah. Who cares if they are not at the 2.25 minutes per call that you'd like to see? Sure, maybe they could be even better if they were a bit more consultative, and you can try to coach accordingly. But at the end of the day, what do you really want?

Of course, if the rep is banging out a call at 1.5 minutes and he or she is *not* getting the sales, dive into your monitoring. Find out why the calls are so short. Listen and learn. Then do something about it.

Revenues

Revenues are different from sales. You can have high sales volume but low revenues. This probably means your rep is selling the easy stuff. Just as the other indicators serve as flags, look at revenues and determine if that flag is red, yellow, or green.

Ratios

I like ratios, and so should you. They give you perspective. But they are not absolutes either. These are the ratios to watch for.

1.   Dials to DMCs

The ratio of dials to DMCs reveals the typical number of dials it takes to reach a decision maker. If it takes 60 dials to reach 20 decision makers, their ratio is 33 percent.

The ratio only becomes helpful when you can trend it relative to others in your department. If, over time and over several reps, you determine that 60 dials generally yields 20 decision makers, you can feel reasonably comfortable using 33 percent as a benchmark. But remember, you are dealing with averages. Some reps may have a higher contact rate, and others may have a lower contact rate. Skill and luck play a role.

If your telesales rep is *not* achieving this ratio, it simply tells you to monitor and find out why. But if your rep is not achieving this ratio and is 138 percent to objective, tune in and find out why he or she is selling so well. But don't come down too hard if they aren't up to the objectives you set. Got it?

2.   DMC to sale

Put another way, this is your sales ratio. It means the number of sales achieved versus the number of clients spoken to—the higher the percentage, the higher the close rate.

This too, is a handy ratio to lend perspective. If a rep has a high DMC rate but a low sales rate, it might suggest that monitoring is necessary to assess the selling skill level. But take this with a grain or two of salt, as well. Some sales have longer cycles, and just because the rep is talking to a decision maker, it does not necessarily mean there is a sales opportunity.

Here again, I offer the caution that numbers are only indicators, not absolutes.

CHAPTER FIVE

Step #4: Feedback

L et's face it; feedback is the real star of the show. While the other three steps are critical, vital, and necessary, they all culminate at this point. Feedback is what your rep hears. Feedback is the direction and focus that you provide so the rep can make a change or continue to progress. So it makes sense that we spend a fair bit of time here.

In this chapter:

- Feedback—Revisited and Defined
- Who Should Receive Feedback?
- Who Should Provide Feedback and the Dangers of Third-Party Feedback
- 3 Choices for Where to Provide Feedback
- The Rule of 2: When to Provide Feedback
- Don't Make This Feedback Mistake
- How *Not* to Provide Feedback
- How to Provide Meaningful, Effective, and Behavior-Changing Feedback

- Assessment Feedback: The Most Common and Worst Type of Feedback
- Developmental Feedback: The 2 Most *Effective* Ways to Provide Behavior Changing Feedback
- The 3 Feedback Techniques You Should Avoid
- Directive Feedback

Feedback—Revisited and Defined

Formally defined, **feedback is the process used to recognize to-standard and not to-standard performance and the steps taken to encourage, modify, or improve selling behavior**.

More colloquially, feedback is where the rubber meets the road. This is when you articulate your observations and comments to your telesales rep based on your monitoring and your analysis. Feedback is engaging your rep in a dialogue—sharing your thoughts and listening to theirs.

At the risk of being obvious, this is where the process of change begins. Feedback makes the rep AWARE of the behavior. Feedback provides specific focus on the behavior that needs to be maintained, modified, changed, or tweaked.

Without feedback, reps can drift merrily along, not realizing they are failing—or if they realize they are failing, not knowing what to do to change the situation.

We provide feedback because it is intuitive. Precisely how we provide feedback is not so intuitive. Not only is it ineffective to give feedback poorly or inadequately, but also it can be counterproductive and damaging.

Who Should Receive Feedback?

At the risk of stating the obvious, you provide feedback to those whom you have monitored. Precisely who you monitor is the real question and was discussed on page 66 (The "A", "B", "C" and "R" of monitoring).

If you have the time and inclination you can monitor, analyze and provide feedback to all your telephone reps. If you have a small team this might be manageable. But the majority of telesales managers don't have the luxury of a lot of spare time. Time is precious; it is an investment. Therefore, the time you dedicate to coaching (and subsequent feedback) should be spent on those reps who offer you and your company the greatest potential of return on your investment.

Who Should Provide Feedback and the Dangers of Third-Party Feedback

Do you want to ruin your coaching program in one or two fell swoops? If you're not careful, you can.

When we discussed monitoring a couple of chapters ago, we indicated that anyone can monitor a call—managers, other reps, VPs, owners, the accountant, and customer service reps. Anyone can monitor for whatever reason.

But not everyone can provide feedback.

There are two cardinal rules regarding feedback. If you want your coaching program to maintain its integrity, pay close attention to the following.

Rule #1: Only those who have been trained as a coach can provide feedback.

Once you implement a coaching program into your telesales department, you must make certain that the effort is not sullied by well-intentioned others within your company.

This is best explained with an example that I am certain many of you can appreciate. After I had helped develop and implement a coaching program at a firm, the owner proudly waltzed through the telesales department like an admiral on a ship. He had not participated in the training program for the coaches, so he was not aware of the coaching processes.

The owner felt the compelling need to provide off-the-cuff coaching tips, techniques, and recommendations to a half a dozen or so telesales reps. The problem was that these suggestions were not only anecdotal, but also they were often contrary to the standards that were provided in training. These telesales reps were given coaching tips that were wrong and ineffective, but who were they to argue otherwise?

But it was the managers who suffered the most. They were now placed in the awkward position of having to re-coach the reps and do so in a politically sensitive manner.

The moral of the story is if you are going to implement a coaching program, make certain everyone is onboard relative to the feedback process. This means especially owners and executives who may unintentionally cause chaos and confusion.

But it's not just executives you need to worry about. It's other telesales reps, too. You're bound to discover one or two reps who feel the need to give neighborly advice to others on the floor. Often they dispense their wisdom to unsuspecting rookies who don't know any better. In any case, the feedback, though well intentioned, can be damaging. It can also create sensitivities among your reps.

Therefore, communicate to your organization that any feedback is welcome, but the feedback should be directed only to the manager and not to the telesales reps.

Rule #2: Only the person who monitored the call can provide feedback.

Here's a typical example to illustrate this point. A telesales rep overhears a call that a fellow rep has made to a customer. The eavesdropper thinks he hears an abusive tone used by his mate. At this conjecture, the rep runs over to you and says, "I just heard Jim on a difficult call. His tone got pretty nasty, and I am pretty certain he swore."

So what do you do?

What you don't want to do is zip over to Jim and confront him with the feedback you received from the well-intentioned listener.

This is called third-party feedback. It'll kill your coaching program by creating an atmosphere of "Big Brother is watching." It'll lead to bitter feelings and retaliatory behaviors. Therefore, you must not provide feedback to the rep based on the monitoring of another.

However, you do have a couple of options. If the call was recorded, go back and listen to it. You can analyze the situation and deal with the feedback accordingly. Or you can begin to monitor calls right away to gauge the behavior of the accused rep. Or, if you are really concerned, you can simply say to the rep, "How did that last call go?" Let your rep elaborate. Do not reference the eavesdropper or what that rep had to say.

This rule applies to big situations (such as the example above) and small ones, too. Executives and owners are often the biggest culprits. Most of them learn that they should not provide feedback unless they are trained in coaching techniques, but many of them will rush back to you and say, "I just overhead Mandi's last call, and it is clear that she's not closing. You better go over there and coach her."

What do you do?

Use your common sense, but be aware that if you provide feedback on something you did not hear or observe, you jeopardize the coaching program.

3 Choices for Where to Provide Feedback

Is it possible to augment your feedback by leveraging precisely where you provide feedback?

Yes.

Like monitoring, precisely where you provide the feedback really does impact the quality and impact of your coaching program. When you analyze the calls you have just monitored, think carefully about the location where the feedback will be given. You have three options:

1. The rep's workstation
2. Your workstation
3. A remote and private location

Each has its own pros and cons, but begin by thinking about the rep to whom you're about to provide feedback, the nature of the call you monitored, the nature of the feedback you want to provide, and finally, the past coaching sessions with your rep. Then ask yourself, "What location will have the best impact?"

1. At the rep's workstation

Providing feedback at your rep's workstation has a couple of major advantages. First, it saves you and the rep time and energy. The rep doesn't have to get up and leave to hear your feedback, which makes him or her more productive. It's fast and relatively simple.

Second, providing feedback at your rep's workstation creates the ripple effect. Depending on how workstations are laid out, other reps can overhear the feedback—and you can bet they'll eavesdrop—and benefit from your comment. Call it vicarious learning. An additional advantage is that your coaching will be seen as constructive and aboveboard. Consequently, it will be a positive activity on the floor.

There can be disadvantages. Again, depending on the layout of your floor, feedback could be distracting to others who are nearby, and it might impact their productivity and effectiveness. Another disadvantage is that other reps can interrupt you with questions, which can dilute the quality and effectiveness of your feedback with the rep. Finally, depending on personality and character of the telephone rep you might get into situations where discussions could be awkward. For instance, if the rep tends to get defensive, you might not want others to be listening in.

2. At your workstation or desk

The primary advantage to providing feedback at your workstation is that it might be convenient for you. If you have the benefit of a door, it can create privacy for awkward situations, reduce interruptions, and eliminate distractions from others.

You can also use your workstation to create a little drama and enhance the coaching moment. Suppose you monitor a call from your workstation, and then you call your rep to come to your office for feedback. The rep must get up and leave his or her desk and walk to your office or cubicle. At some level, there's a statement that is being made. If the feedback is constructive, the walk illustrates how important the feedback is. If the feedback is nothing but good news, it accentuates the positive even more so. Many of your other telesales reps will take note of the walk. It has significance, and so it sends a message to the team about the importance of feedback.

3.   At a remote location

A remote location might be a private room other than your office or the rep's desk. Remote locations ensure virtually no interruptions and ensure maximum privacy.

I am not a big fan of remote location feedback because providing feedback should be a positive process, but there are times when it's the best route. In one situation, I worked with an extremely sensitive rep who would literally tear up and verbally withdraw when she received even the most minor feedback. Feedback discussions were embarrassing to her, so we moved to a private room. She was much more receptive.

In many cases, there have been reps who used the feedback session as an opportunity to lament about the company's policies or pricing, or about market conditions, or about the owner, etc. The best policy was to isolate the rep so there wouldn't be an audience. The net result was that the rep tended to listen more closely to the feedback rather than grandstand because he or she did not have an audience.

The Rule of 2: When to Provide Feedback

When to provide feedback is not rocket science. You have two choices:

1. Immediately after monitoring
2. After a delay

However, which option you choose has an element of science to it. Just like choosing the best location, when you provide the feedback might improve the reception of the feedback.

Like everything else, there are pros and cons to each option, and much of your decision will depend on circumstances.

Immediate Feedback

Immediate feedback means providing feedback right after you have monitored and analyzed a call.

The single most important benefit of immediate feedback is that the call is fresh in the mind of the rep, and he or she can apply the feedback immediately after the call. The behavior-change process begins instantly. Additionally, providing feedback immediately saves you time, and it saves the rep time.

Delayed Feedback

As much as I might like immediate feedback, there are times when it is not the best option.

Delayed feedback is provided after a period of time. For example, you might wish to monitor several calls before providing feedback because you are trying to determine if the rep is exhibiting a trend in sales behavior or if the call, or a portion of the call, was a simple aberration.

Delaying the feedback can help you avoid being seen as petty. This is why analysis is so important. Wait a moment or two, and determine if it is worth the immediate time and effort.

Feedback might also be delayed if you're faced with a sensitive issue. Perhaps the rep is frustrated and stressed because he or she is not performing well. Your feedback might overwhelm him or her; it might be wasted because he or she is not in the right frame of mind to process what you've monitored or observed. Be sensitive to the situation. Hold back the feedback.

Perhaps you are somewhat overwhelmed and frustrated with the rep. Perhaps the rep is repeatedly making the same error. Or maybe he or she is deliberately testing your patience (and many do). In that situation, your concern might be that your feedback will move from rational to emotional. In other words, you're not quite certain how well you will deal with the situation. In this case, it is best to take a break. Don't tamper with the coaching process if you think it could possibly take a wrong turn.

Of course, the longer you delay, the harder it will be for the rep to remember the call. Unless you have call-recording capabilities, the call will become hazier by the minute. This means that the feedback will be diluted if the rep does not have a crystal clear memory of the call or the specific skill set to which you will be referring.

Don't Make This Feedback Mistake

Doing something effective is useless if it's done too late. Sometimes we do the same thing in coaching. Here's an illustrative example.

Several of my larger clients gave feedback to their reps on a monthly basis. At the beginning of each month, the telesales reps met with their managers to monitor recorded calls that had been made throughout the prior month. Typically, the managers identified several calls where not to-standard skills or techniques had been used, and provided feedback to help modify and correct the behavior. The calls were fresh in the minds of the reps because, they had been recorded. The feedback was often very good and helpful.

But here's the kicker. Any given call may have occurred one, two, three, or even four weeks earlier!

How astounding is that?

The rep had many weeks in which to repeat the same mistakes over and over at the cost of sales and customer satisfaction. What is more, if the substandard behavior was continuous, the rep would have likely developed a habit that would be harder to modify.

This would be frustrating for you, the rep, and quite possibly, the customer. And who knows what opportunities would have been lost.

How *Not* to Provide Feedback

The 7 Most Destructive Styles of Coaching Feedback

Do you *really* coach your reps, or do you compete with them?

Some managers are not aware of it, but they do a rotten job because they actually compete with their sales reps rather than provide constructive feedback to help them change and modify their behavior to sell more.

Though they may be well intentioned, competitive coaches do more harm than good. Apart from doing little to improve the sales behavior of the rep, they can inadvertently cause resentment, foster frustration, and destroy confidence.

What is a competitive coach?

The competitive coach is a manager whose feedback tends to elevate his or her own knowledge and expertise in selling while diminishing the effort or the skill of the sales rep. Often oblivious to this behavior, the competitive coach tends to point how he or she would have done things differently and, of course, better, which belittles the rep.

Here are some typical examples of competitive coaching styles.

1.   The tell style

The competitive coach tends to a have a "let me tell you" approach to feedback. These coaches are direct and often blunt in their remarks.

"You didn't close."

"You missed the buying signal."

"Next time, practice your presentation."

Certainly, there are times when the direct approach is effective, but the problem with the tell style is that it rarely helps the sales rep alter his or her selling behavior. Instead, it reveals flaws, which embarrasses or annoys the rep.

2. Chide, deride, and kid style

Some managers tend to coach their reps by chiding, kidding, or deriding. For instance, they may say:

> "Kelly, what the heck was *that*?"

> "Cathy, are you kidding me? A seven-year-old could have closed that one."

The manager doesn't necessarily mean to be harsh or demeaning, but that's the net result. Most reps get defensive, silently or vocally.

3. Nitpick style

Very competitive coaches often feel that they *must* give some sort of critical feedback even if the call was exceptionally good. They will find something—anything—that could be better or improved. Again, this approach tends to raise the manager's perceived value, intelligence, and savvy of himself or herself, if only because the manager lowers the skill or ability of the rep. Good coaches know that if there are no flaws, there is no need to make them up.

4. Sandwich style

Competitive coaches often use the sandwich technique of feedback, which has been taught for years but is really a discouraging model. This technique states that constructive feedback should be sandwiched between a couple positive comments. For example,

> "Jen, that opening statement was really good, but I'm afraid the questioning and qualifying needs some work. You didn't

> really get to the heart of the client's needs. Mind you, you did attempt a close."

The "but" is the real killer. The beleaguered rep, Jen, hears the positive remark, but she is waiting for the other shoe to drop the moment the word "but" comes out of the manager's mouth. In an instant, the positive comment is negated. Or, the rep hears the positive remarks, congratulates herself, and doesn't hear the constructive. Rare is the rep who can emotionally separate the two types of feedback.

The good coach gives either constructive feedback or positive feedback and lets the call stand on those merits.

5.   The rhetorical style

Like sports coaches, competitive sales coaches sometimes use rhetorical questions as a means of pumping up reps and giving them feedback.

> "You want to be winner, don't you?"

> "You want to close 'em, right?"

> "You don't want to stay at the bottom of the heap, do you?"

> "Why didn't you ask for the referral?"

The manager is not looking for answers; he or she is pointing out the mistake and trusting that it will dramatically improve sales performance. The fact of the matter is most reps simply endure the rhetoric and go on to make the same mistake.

Good coaching is a two-way street. A good manager and coach asks questions and waits for feedback. This interactive approach helps the rep understand and learn.

6.   Personal-anecdotes style

Many sales managers are former sales reps, and chances are they were good sales reps. Consequently, their coaching is spotted with all sorts of personal anecdotes such as,:

> "When I was on the phone, I used the direct close."

> "I remember a similar customer, and here's what I did to close that twenty-thousand-dollar deal."

Sure, there are times when personal gems might have some value, but mostly they are war stories that tell the rep how good the manager was. The implication is that the rep could be that good if only he or she followed your advice.

7.   Heaping style

The final coaching style is the manager who heaps on the feedback to such an extent that the information becomes too overwhelming for the rep. This often occurs with rookies, where the entire call is weak and the manager provides feedback on everything from the planning, the opening, the questioning, the presentation, the objection handling, and the close. The telesales rep is left lost and discouraged.

A good coach focuses on one or two areas that require constructive feedback. It's best to let the rep learn and master these areas before moving on to the rest of the call.

Competitive managers do not have a nefarious plan to sabotage their sales reps. Most competitive managers are not effective coaches simply because they have never learned how to provide behavior-changing feedback.

How to Provide Meaningful, Effective, and Behavior-Changing Feedback

This is what the coaching process boils down to: providing the feedback that will ultimately lead to a change in your reps' selling behavior. It is here, through your words, that the rep will take what you say, process it, and either apply your feedback or dismiss it.

So what this really means is that you can monitor until you're blue in the face, and you can analyze for hours, but at the end of it all, none of it will matter if you foul up the feedback process. Precisely how you give feedback will determine the success of your program.

Assessment Feedback: The Most Common and Worst Type of Feedback

Assessment feedback is overwhelmingly the most common form of feedback employed by telesales managers. Regrettably, it is probably the worst type of feedback on the face of the earth. I have touched on this point before but it is vital to review it.

Assessment feedback is characterized by the manager *telling* the telesales rep what was heard. It is evaluative in that it points out what *was not done correctly*. Sometimes a score is provided based on a weighted scale. Here's an example.

"Amanda, I just monitored that last call. Your opening statement was weak. It didn't have a benefit. Also, you didn't really question. You pitched. The prospect wasn't involved. And speaking of a pitch, it was unclear. I give this call a C minus."

Of course, you would never be so brutal in your feedback, right?

This example is a bit contrived, but it is used to illustrate the nature of assessment feedback. The trouble with assessment feedback is that it is so darn quick and easy to give. It deals directly and specifically with the monitored behavior, so there is no quibbling and confusion. It saves time and effort. The manager feels he or she has done a good coaching job and can move on to the next call or the next rep. All in all, assessment feedback is convenient, which explains why it is so common.

But convenient is not always effective.

Note in the example above that Amanda is not part of the feedback process. She is the recipient. The feedback may be accurate, but it lacks a constructive quality. It assesses the call in general, but it does not offer solutions or recommendations to help the rep improve or develop or learn much from the experience. As such, modification of behavior rarely takes place. Assessment feedback is not linked to a standard, which can make it rather arbitrary and subjective.

Now, assessment feedback can work in certain circumstances. For example, if you have a rep who knows the standards and has been coached repeatedly on the specific skill or technique, assessment feedback might be the best strategy. But in general, assessment feedback puts people on the defensive, and at some level, they close their minds to what is being said.

So what does this really mean?

It means that the analysis phase of the coaching process should be used to determine the best possible approach to giving feedback.

Developmental Feedback: The 2 Most *Effective* Ways to Provide Behavior Changing Feedback

"What's the best way to give feedback so that the rep wants to make the effort to change?"

This is the number one question I get in every coaching seminar.

Without a doubt, bar none, the best form of feedback is developmental feedback.

As the name implies, developmental feedback develops and nurtures the rep. It provides the rep with specifics on how to improve or how to continue to improve. As such, it has a positive quality. Reps do not feel defensive, so they are open to the remarks. The feedback is encouraging, and the rep feels good about making an effort.

There are two types of developmental feedback: One-Minute Praise and Socratic.

Developmental Style #1: One-minute praise feedback

Sometimes, simple is best. Here is an easy and effective feedback technique that can pay huge dividends in modifying the behavior in your reps and helping them to sell more. It's been around for well over twenty years, but the principle is timeless, and it is perfect for the world of telesales.

Back in the 1980s, author Ken Blanchard and Spencer Johnson wrote a book called *The One Minute Manager*. It was an instant hit around the world. Easy and entertaining to read, the book was based on the premise that most workers (including telesales reps) do not receive enough positive praise from their bosses. In fact, some researchers have discovered that negative feedback is given five times more often than positive feedback.

The authors set out to deal with the issue. Their approach was stunningly simple.

Blanchard and Johnson maintained that if people received more recognition for their positive contributions, they were more likely to repeat it. Their approach was to implement what they called "one-minute praise." As the name suggests, one-minute praise was designed to give quick, positive praise in less than a minute. In other words, give the rep a pat on the back, an "attaboy," a sincere and direct compliment, and then you should move on. Don't lather it. Provide the praise, and let it stand on its own merit.

How to provide one-minute praise to telesales reps

Providing one-minute praise is as easy as pie and consists of two parts.

Part I: Describe the behavior monitored.

The first component is to describe the positive behavior that has been monitored or observed. Blanchard and Johnson maintain you must be as specific as possible for the praise to have the best impact. It makes complete sense. When you monitor a superb skill or technique, describe precisely what you heard because the rep is more likely to repeat it.

Part II: Provide brief praise.

The second component is to praise that behavior. Compliment it. Acknowledge it. It is the sincere compliment that warms the spirit and makes the rep feel good. But be brief. If you go overboard, the praise might sound a bit contrived and lose its impact.

Here's an example.

> "Kelly, I was monitoring that call to Mr. Sanchez. Well done! The way you handled his 'I am in a meeting' knee-jerk objection was textbook! You paused, you ignored it, and used the one-quick-question technique. It worked to a tee. You delivered it with confidence, and it worked. Keep it up."

Notice how specific the praise was. The manager reinforces the three steps involved in handling the knee-jerk objection. In this manner, the technique is further reinforced and supported. And remember, if the praise is given at the rep's workstation, everyone within hearing distance listens to it and is reminded of the specifics of the standard for handling a knee-jerk objection. Kind of a double-whammy benefit!

> "Mike, you did an awesome job with that opening statement. It had all five components, but what was most effective was the benefit statement you used. It really caught the prospect's ear and got her engaged. Excellent work!"

In this example, the manager focuses on praising the benefit statement. He does this because the majority of reps tend to forget or ignore this portion of the five steps involved in a good opening statement.

(Remember, this is a standard I have created for opening statements; yours might be different.) By emphasizing this particular area of the opener, he is rewarding the rep for good behavior and encouraging him or her to repeat it.

> "Erin, that call was probably the best I've heard since you started. You followed the entire call-guide process from stem to stern. Keep that up, and you'll be making sales in no time flat."

In the above example, it is obvious that Erin did not get a sale. It is also implied that she is a rookie. Praise was given despite not getting the sale because the manager is seeking to praise Erin's commitment to follow the process.

The above feedback examples take fewer than thirty seconds to deliver. It's that easy, and it can be immensely effective.

Who should receive one-minute praise?

Every rep can benefit from a pat on the back. Who doesn't like a well-meant compliment?

But one-minute praise is especially effective with rookies. Reps fresh out of training need as much support as they can get. Their heads are crammed full of product knowledge, skill knowledge, and technical knowledge. They are going to be overwhelmed, and they will make mistakes.

If you focus only on corrective feedback, you can frustrate them. "Oh, there's so much to learn! I'll never get the hang of this!" They may not tell you that, but they are thinking that. So give them small victories. Praise the most fundamental of skills in the early stages of development.

Nothing is too trivial at this point. The praise lets them know you are in their corner and there to help. The coaching process is then positioned as extremely positive. And above all, it will make them more open and receptive to your corrective feedback.

Don't sully the moment.

Whatever you do, do not combine your one-minute praise with corrective feedback. I call this sandwich feedback. More on this later, but here's an example.

> "Todd, I just monitored that call. Your opening statement was great. You hit all five components, and you delivered them with conviction. Keep it up. Now, your questioning still needs a bit of work."

The praise starts off with a bang, very encouraging. But what happens next? By adding the comment about questioning, the positive nature of the praise is immediately diluted and maybe even lost. The poor rep is not certain of the real message. Is it a positive or a negative? Don't kid yourself into thinking that the rep understands the singular nature of each comment. The vast majority will key into either one part of the message or the other.

One-minute praise is about praise and nothing else. It does not matter if the call you monitored was a complete shamble. If your objective is to encourage the rep, find something to praise, and leave it at that. You will have plenty of opportunity to provide corrective feedback down the line. Don't sully the moment.

The danger of one-minute praise

Just when you thought one-minute praise ranked right up there with sliced bread, here is a caution. Too much one-minute praise can destroy the integrity of the process.

It might seem odd, but if you use one-minute praise too often, it loses its effect. After a period of time, reps begin to recognize that the praise is being doled out right, left, and center. Initially, especially if they are rookies, it warms and delights them. But over time, it becomes overdone, and they sense that. At that moment, the praise turns from positive to indifferent. After that, it turns from indifferent to farcical.

Regrettably, reps do become cynical. It's a fact. You know it as well as I do. They will joke around with one another and say, "Oh, here comes the boss with her daily dose of praise." (This is a real comment.)

Another odd behavior is the "yesterday's luxuries become today's necessities" syndrome. Reps who are accustomed to praise can become hurt, annoyed, or suspicious when they do not get the high-five compliment. Weird, huh?! But that comes from conditioning. If you condition reps with too much praise, it becomes expected. And if they don't get it, they can become petulant, not unlike spoiled children.

Another peculiar element of one-minute praise is that managers sometimes use it inappropriately and confuse their reps. For example, a savvy rep, who consistently exceeds her objectives, rarely benefits from praise for a skill or technique that is obvious and expected. You expect a veteran rep to have good closing skills. So providing one-minute praise for a second-nature skill loses its impact. In fact, it probably confounds the rep ("Like, what was that all about?")

This is not to say that talented reps can't benefit from one-minute praise. They can. But look for some unique achievement and provide them with sincere and meaningful praise.

A matter of degree

One-minute praise is a powerful feedback tool to help change behavior. Its effectiveness depends on the degree to which you use it. The reps become immune to its modifying power when it's used too often. Use it too little, and you won't get the benefits it has to offer.

The best rule of thumb is to think before you apply it. Remember the analysis phase of coaching. As mentioned, rookies crave it and need it. But your veteran reps may be a different story. Think before you act. It's easy to do. Just apply common sense.

Developmental style #2: Socratic feedback

While one-minute praise has it merits, Socratic feedback is unquestionably the most effective of the two developmental methods for the vast majority of reps and situations. It is relatively easy to learn, and it is powerfully effective because it gets the telesales reps *involved* in the feedback process. It gets them to take personal ownership when it comes to changing their sales behavior. By contrast, one-minute praise tends to be a one way process.

What is it?

Socratic feedback gets its name from Socrates, the Greek philosopher and teacher. Socrates's method of education and feedback was to use questioning rather than providing direct instruction. He would pose questions to his students that were designed to get them to think.

Socrates felt that his pupils were more likely to take ownership for the information if they derived the answers themselves. He also felt they would internalize the information and retain it if they came to the conclusion on their own.

It's a powerful concept that has long been used as a teaching technique, and it is absolutely superb as a means of providing constructive feedback to a telesales rep.

Why does it work so well?

The beauty of Socratic feedback is that, when it is done well, the telesales rep actually provides his or her own feedback. In effect, the reps coach themselves based on the answers to the questions posed by their coaches. The coach's role is simply to direct the reps to the monitored behavior. Let them conduct their own personal analysis. When they do the analysis of a call or a technique, and when they arrive at a process by which to modify their behavior, they take personal ownership. It is their analysis. It is their game plan.

When they take personal ownership (i.e., when they internalize what they have said and what actions are necessary), they are more likely to implement the change. In a sense, Socratic feedback takes you, the manager, out of the equation and puts them smack dab in the middle of it. Your questions point the reps in the right direction, but their personal answers remove any subjectivity from the equation. It's not the subjective opinion or feedback of the manager that they are processing, it is theirs. In the minds of most reps, this makes the feedback fair and equitable. There is no emotion attached to it. Consequently, it is an easier pill to swallow.

The 5 steps to Socratic feedback

Socratic feedback consists of five relatively simple steps.

The 5 Step Socratic Feedback Model

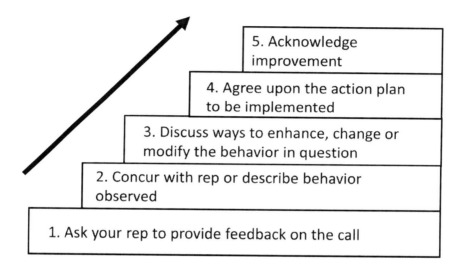

5. Acknowledge improvement

4. Agree upon the action plan to be implemented

3. Discuss ways to enhance, change or modify the behavior in question

2. Concur with rep or describe behavior observed

1. Ask your rep to provide feedback on the call

Step #1: Ask rep to provide feedback on contact.

Instead of pointing out the not to-standard behavior, the trick here is to get the rep to identify the behavior. You do this by asking,

> "Aaron, I have been monitoring the last few calls you have made. Tell me, how do you think they've been going?"

This open-ended question is a nifty way to begin the Socratic process. There is no judgment rendered. There is no criticism implied. It is broad enough that the rep can comment as he or she sees fit. In this manner, the rep is not put on the spot. And by the way, this technique could be used to provide positive feedback as easily as corrective feedback.

Here's another example, assuming that the manager is plugged in beside the rep at her workstation.

> "Jennifer, how do you feel that call went?"

Again, this is an open-ended question. The rep can do an analysis on the entire call or on a single part of the call. The manager could also be more specific and to the point by saying,

> "Jennifer, how do you feel your response to that objection— 'send me some literature'—went?"

In this case, the manager gets to the main area of focus right off the bat. Whatever the case, the rep is the one who will do the analysis.

2. Describe the behavior observed.

You may not even have to do this step. If you've set firm standards, and if you coach often, your reps will be able to quickly and effectively identify the areas that may need work. That's the real beauty of the process. So, when asked how the call went, the rep might respond,

> "My opening is okay, but I keep stumbling when they toss me a knee-jerk objection. I get flustered when they say 'I'm in a meeting' or 'I'm busy right now.'"

Assuming this was the area that you wanted to discuss, notice how the rep has identified it on his or her own. You didn't have to say a word other than to ask the question. You don't look like the heavy, and you certainly are not criticizing him or her. Again, this takes the emotional resistance out of the feedback process. The rep doesn't feel defensive and is more open to the process because he's not dealing with hurt feelings.

Of course, it would be absolutely great for you if all your reps were able to quickly and efficiently identify the specific areas where they might need feedback. But that doesn't always happen. Some reps will be oblivious to their behavior, while others will still be retentive about doing their own self-analysis.

In those situations, you need to use questions to point the rep to the behavior, and you need to use questions to determine if the rep truly understands the standard for a given skill or technique. So let's return to Jennifer, who is oblivious to her behavior.

Manager: "Jennifer, how do you feel your response to that objection—'send me some literature'—went?"

Jennifer: "I think it went well. The prospect seemed interested and wanted more information, so I will get it to her and then follow up."

Manager: "Okay. Let me ask you, what did we learn in training about a smokescreen objection?"

Jennifer: "Ummm . . . it's an objection that comes near the end of the call, and it is often false; it hides something else."

Manager: "Good. That's it exactly. What were some of the classic smokescreen objections that we learned?"

Jennifer: "Let's see. 'Let me think about it;' 'I need to talk to my boss;' 'call me next week' . . ."

Manager: "And . . . ?"

Jennifer: "Send me something in the mail, or e-mail me, or fax me."

Manager: "Right. And so . . . ?"

Jennifer: "Well . . . I think he really wants to see something in writing. I could hear it in his voice. I think he was sincere."

Manager: "You could be right. But remember what we said about the dual nature of smokescreens; they could be real, or they could be hiding something else. And because of that, we developed a process to determine if it's real or otherwise. Do you remember that?"

Jennifer: "I think so."

Manager: "What was the process we laid out to determine if the objection is real or not?"

Jennifer: "We are supposed to empathize with the client. Say something like, 'I understand.' And then we are supposed to question or clarify to determine if the objection is real or not. Once we know for certain, we can respond."

Manager: "Well done. That's exactly right."

In this example, notice how the manager was supportive. This is a version of the one-minute praise approach. When Jennifer answered verification questions correctly, the manager provided a positive remark such as "good" or "well done." The manager did not layer it on. Instead, she used the praise to encourage the rep to continue the analysis. The praise positions the feedback as positive and lightly handled.

Also note that the manager could have easily flipped to citing the steps that identify the smokescreen. By patiently questioning Jennifer, she identifies that Jennifer knows the process but did not apply it. That's typical. Reps forget. In this case, Jennifer may have believed the client wanted more information on paper. But that's not the SOP for handling smokescreens. Consequently, the manager delved further to make certain Jennifer knew the steps. It is obvious, then, that Jennifer doesn't need training; she needs reminding. And Jennifer reminded herself!

3.   Discuss ways to enhance or change the behavior.

Something has caused Jennifer not to use the technique. The manager could get into a long discussion about why, but that's time-consuming and not always productive. Feedback is a quick process, not a belabored discussion. At this stage, use questioning to develop a game plan for modifying behavior.

Manager: "Okay, Jennifer, what do you think you can do to help remember the technique?"

Jennifer: "I guess I could practice more."

Manager: "Yep, that'll really help. But what else could you do or use to help prompt you?"

Jennifer: "Ah, I'm not certain."

Manager: "Do you remember the job aid we created, the objections chart?"

Jennifer: "Oh, yes! It's in my workbook."

Manager: "What could you do to make that more prominent at your desk?"

Jennifer: "Maybe redo it or tear it out and hang it up so that I can use it like a cheat sheet."

Manager: "Exactly. Well done."

Here again, the manager could have easily reminded her rep about the objections chart and told her to post it. It would have been faster. But the point behind the Socratic process is to have the reps develop the game plan because when they do, they take greater ownership. It is more likely to get done. Additionally, the integrity of the coaching process is maintained. Coaching is seen as positive.

At this stage, the manager has another option: a quick role play session with the rep. For instance, the manager might say, "Okay, Jennifer, let's role play. I say to you, "E-mail me some literature." Using the objections handling process, how would you reply?" This is a powerful way to reinforce the skill set and get Jennifer more comfortable with the technique. It also verifies to the manager that Jennifer can effectively apply the process.

4.   Agree upon the action plan implemented.

The fourth step is designed to ensure that both the manager and the rep understand what needs to happen.

Manager: "Okay, so you'll either redo the chart or post the one from your workbook, right?"

Jennifer: "Right."

Manager: "And when can you get that done?"

Jennifer: "I'll have it done after lunch."

Manager: "Sounds like a plan."

This is an important step. In this example, a time frame has been established. It creates a minor degree of pressure on the rep. This is good stress. It gets the rep going in the right direction. It is also clear what is expected.

Sometimes the action plan is simpler; the rep agrees to apply the technique right away. A job aid might not be necessary or even applicable. Either way, the manager is simply seeking confirmation that the standard for a given skill will be applied.

5.   Acknowledge improvement.

In many ways, the final step is maybe the most important step in Socratic feedback.

In many coaching situations feedback is presented, and it is unintentionally left at that. In other words, the manager has done his job with that call or that rep, and then the manager moves on to something else. The trouble is that the rep often thinks the same way. The manager has given the feedback. The rep has listened. And the rep thinks, *Now let's move on to the next call.*

In an odd way, the feedback can be forgotten almost immediately. It's human nature. But the way to make the feedback stick is to let the rep know that the coaching doesn't ever stop. By coming back shortly—that same day or the next—and providing acknowledgment of the change in behavior, the manager sends the message that he or she really does expect a change. It tells the reps that going back to their old behavior is not acceptable.

So in Jennifer's case, the manager would come by her desk sometime after lunch to see if the chart had been posted.

Manager: "Hey, Jennifer. I see you have the chart pinned to your cubicle. Have you had a chance to use it?"

In just a few seconds, Jennifer realizes her manager is inspecting and verifying that the action item was completed. It tells her that it was important to the manager, and therefore, it should be important to the rep.

Suppose Jennifer doesn't have the chart posted.

Manager: "Hey, Jennifer. Where's your chart?"

Notice the question-based approach. There is no recrimination. It's a simple question, but it speaks volumes. Jennifer will stutter and start and maybe toss out an excuse or two. But in any event, she'll know that the feedback wasn't given lightly. She'll realize that there are expectations to be met. You can bet that she'll post that chart within the next half hour. And it can't hurt for the manager to drop by again at the end of the day to praise Jennifer for posting the chart.

Truthfully, inspecting the change of behavior can be tough and time-consuming. You will not be able to do it all the time. But you can make a note of your feedback in your files (or on your yellow monitoring sheet), and the next time you monitor, you can determine if the rep has applied the techniques you agreed upon.

Feedback Techniques You Should Avoid

There are four types of feedback you should avoid: the rated, the sandwich, the overload, and the constructive only. As you'll see, these forms of feedback confuse the rep and do little to modify the behavior.

1.   Avoid the rated feedback

I touched on this earlier. Rated feedback is where you rate a call using a numeric scale (e.g., 1 to 5 with 5 being the highest). In some cases, different parts of the call are weighted to indicate they are more significant than others. Ultimately you end up with scores for various parts of the call or a score for the entire call or both.

Everyone under the sun hates rated calls (unless they have fabulous marks) because the rating is subjective. They are not grounded in a standard, so the evaluation is completely arbitrary. Therein lies the problem from a feedback perspective. Any feedback that has a numeric evaluation attached to it means that the feedback is arbitrary and inconsistent. Where you might rate a rep's opening statement 5, I might rate it a 3. Who is right? Worse, you might rate it a 5 one day and then a 3 the following week simply because you forgot the feedback. Your poor telephone rep is left frustrated and no further ahead because he or she knows that you are simply expressing an opinion.

(In fact, I have seen situations where one manager gave the rep a rating of 87 and provided feedback to improve the score. The rep applied the techniques he got from the feedback session but had another manager monitor the call. The second manager gave him a rating of 79. Go figure!)

2.   Avoid the sandwich feedback.

As mentioned earlier, the sandwich technique has been around for a long time. Constructive feedback is sandwiched between two pieces of positive feedback. Here's a typical example.

> "Angie, your opening was pretty good. It seemed to get
> the prospect's attention, but your questioning was like an

interrogation with all those closed-ended questions. Now, you did a good job in handling the 'e-mail me something' objection."

Think about it. Is it a good-news message? Or is it a not-so-good message? Proponents of this type of feedback would like you to believe that a sales rep is a rational, level-headed individual who can see the balanced nature of the feedback.

And some will. But most won't.

In fact, the overwhelming majority of sales reps key into the constructive feedback. This is not necessarily a bad thing. The feedback helps focus on the behavior that requires modification. The problem is, the good, encouraging feedback is completely squandered. The rep ignores it or finds it false, a means of softening the blow, so to speak. So, what that really means is that the good behavior is not bolstered. And afterward, every time the rep hears some good feedback, he sits there and waits for the inevitable "but" to fall like an axe.

> "Your presentation was really great, Trent. You covered all the points well, but you didn't close the sale. You left the client dangling."

That "but" is a killer word. It can destroy your entire feedback session in less than a second. Can you think of anything more discouraging?

The other side of the coin when you use sandwich technique is that not all reps will hear the constructive feedback. Some reps will hear only the positive remarks and utterly ignore the constructive feedback. It's almost like they keep score and rationalize their behavior. ("Gee I had two good pieces of feedback, so that beats the one piece of critical feedback. I must be doing well; I'm ahead of the game.") This *will* happen silently and often. It is human nature. (How many times have you heard that?!)

What to do?

The answer is simple. When you present feedback, either focus on the great things the rep did and give him or her unconditional praise, or focus exclusively on the behavior that needs work or modification. Don't do both. You'll confuse the rep and sabotage your coaching program.

Remember, coaching is an ongoing process. You'll have plenty of time to provide feedback. When it's time for positive feedback, give it completely and without any strings attached. When it's time for constructive feedback, give it honestly and objectively, and don't gloss over it.

3. Avoid overload feedback.

Overload feedback is as the name implies; it overloads the rep with too much feedback. It's like stuffing a five-pound bag with ten pounds of sand; you'll end up bursting the bag and losing everything.

Overloading often occurs when coaching rookies. Fresh from their training, the rookies get on the phone, and promptly ignore or partially ignore every standard you set. This is very typical, and it's to be expected.

But the manager unwittingly feels the compelling need to point out all the behaviors that were not to-standard.

> "Pat, I just monitored that call. Wow! Where to begin? First, the opening statement is weak because you did not provide a benefit. Your questioning was, well, a little weak. You're still learning, I know. The presentation wasn't too bad, except

that you did not summarize your points with a benefit. Then you left the client dangling by not attempting a close. And lastly, you did not arrange a follow-up date and time. So work on all that, will ya?"

Of course, this is just a simple and rather blunt example. But you get the point; there's one piece of constructive feedback after another. Even if the Socratic method of feedback were used, the rep would be thoroughly overwhelmed and discouraged. The rep doesn't even know where to begin with all this. The feedback gets lost and loses any impact it might have had.

Limit your feedback.

The key point is to limit your constructive feedback to one or possibly two areas only. Even if the call was a disaster from beginning to end, don't point that out to the rookie rep, and certainly don't waste your time providing feedback. You will achieve nothing. Help the rep succeed at one skill set or technique at a time. Help him or her "divide and conquer." After the rep has mastered one standard, move on to the next. You have plenty of time.

4.   Avoid only constructive feedback.

The final type of feedback to avoid is providing *only* constructive feedback. Even if you use Socratic feedback, and even if you limit your feedback to only one specific standard, skill, technique or process, you can *still* discourage your rep. Imagine yourself as a rep, and every time the manager walked to your desk, he brought only corrective feedback. What would that do to you?

Socratic feedback makes learning easier and helps modify the rep's behavior. But if it is a repeated process, it tends to wear thin. The resolve of many reps will falter. They'll feel discouragement. At that point, no matter how sensitive you are in your feedback, the rep will begin to resist your feedback.

How do you minimize this? Give positive feedback every now and then.

Find something, anything, and give the telephone reps something to rally around. Even if the calls you're monitoring are substandard, find something good or effective and provide positive feedback. New reps need victories. They need success. They need to feel that progress is being made at some level. These victories are like building blocks. If the rep builds a solid foundation on victories, he or she can move forward and build further.

This may seem a little contrary to the suggestions made in the sandwich method, but there's a spin to it. In the sandwich technique, the manager confuses the rep by providing *both* constructive and positive feedback at the same time. The difference here is that *only* positive feedback is provided about the call or series of calls. There is no "but" inserted anywhere. Obviously, this is where one-minute praise kicks in.

> "Todd, you absolutely nailed that presentation. It was clear, concise, and convincing. Good job. Keep it up."

But you can also use the Socratic approach to provide praise.

Manager: "Rochelle, I have been monitoring your last few calls. How do you think your opening statements have been going?"

Rochelle: "Oh, I don't know. Not too good. I seem to be stumbling and bumbling a bit."

Manager: "On the contrary, I think they've been superb. You've hit all the key parts, and you've been consistent with every call. Did you notice, on your last call, how Mr. Howard paused and bit and then said, 'Go on.'"

Rochelle: "Yeah. Actually I did. I thought he was going to say he wasn't interested."

Manager: "And what happened?"

Rochelle: "Well. He didn't agree to the webinar or the follow-up call, so I guess it was a bust."

Manager: "No. That's not what I'm talking about. What happened after the pause?"

Rochelle: "He answered my questions, and I had a chance to present the offer."

Manager: "Right! And all that occurred because you had an opening statement that caught his attention. You won't get a sale every time. No one expects that. But what you did is you created an opportunity. That starts with the opening statement. Yours was good. Keep it up."

Telesales reps will be full of self-doubt when learning new techniques. They often become their own worst critics and begin to feed themselves with negative self-talk. You have to preempt the tendency of reps to beat themselves up. You do that by giving them praise even when the rest of call might be a disaster.

Again, you will have plenty of time to give constructive feedback. Let the good news story seep in. Come back twenty minutes later, and work on questioning or presentation. But for a little while, let the rep bask in the glow of your praise.

Supportive feedback is a technique you must master if you are serious about modifying behavior. It is not absolutely perfect; there are reps who will resist it and ignore the approach. But overall, supportive feedback has the most significant impact on the majority of telesales reps. So use it.

Directive Feedback

Directive feedback is the second type of feedback that you can use to modify and change the sales behavior of your telesales reps. Unlike supportive, directive feedback is somewhat more traditional in that it tends to emphasize "tell" rather than "ask" in its approach. But unlike traditional coaching models that are completely "tell" oriented, the directive feedback is used with deliberate thought and calculation.

The KITA method of feedback

The most effective type of directive feedback is the KITA.

KITA stands for "Kick in the a—." It's a bit of a crude acronym, but I use it because it completely and utterly describes the feedback process. KITA is meant to get the rep's attention. It is meant to show them you are serious and expect more. It's meant to shake them out of their doldrums, or to use an old expression, to wake up and smell the coffee.

When to use KITA

KITA can be used on anyone, but you'll discover that it's primarily for more seasoned and experienced telesales reps. It is predicated on two assumptions. The first is that repeated—note that word, "repeated"—attempts at Socratic feedback have not been successful. The second is that the sales rep is not succeeding in achieving his or her sales objectives. So, to put it more plainly, your telesales rep is not succeeding and doesn't seem to be doing anything about it despite your attempts to assist him or her. Something is contributing to this behavior. Sometimes it is burnout, but more often it is complacency. In either case, your rep needs to be jolted in order for him or her to respond and take action to modify this behavior.

Who should get KITA

KITA is used almost exclusively for veteran and senior reps. These are reps who *know* how to sell and have *proven* they can sell. They've been around; they've been on the leader board. They tend to be confident, ego-driven people. In effect, they are the superstar players who are in a slump. Traditional Socratic feedback isn't working because below-standard performance is really not about skills and techniques. It's about complacency, laziness, boredom, and a lack of drive or focus. KITA aims to break through these barriers. It's a simple process with three elements.

How to provide KITA

Describe the behavior(s).

You must describe the specific behavior or skill that is impacting the sales results. While the issue is really not about the skill set, the lackluster behavior is usually manifested in a whittling of skills and techniques. The confident, successful rep slowly stops or alters the techniques that made him or her successful. They don't respond to Socratic feedback because they are still riding on the momentum of their past successes.

By focusing on the behavior, you are not directly focusing on the rep as an individual.

Give a little kick.

Your next step is to deliver a little kick in the behind to get them to turn their heads and say to themselves, "Hey, he really means it." The little kick is often the tone of your voice. You want a mix of surprise and disappointment. In addition, the little kick is more rhetorical than it is a discussion. You don't really want to debate the issue. That's already been done during the Socratic phase. It wasn't working. Your feedback is more a one-way statement.

Aim the kick at the ego.

Finally—and this is vital—you must appeal to their ego, their sense of pride. Again, this is very critical. A good KITA is really a backhanded compliment. You seek to remind the rep that he or she is or was good or great but is not performing to that standard of excellence you've come to expect. You want to rally them by reminding them of their greatness. This can help stir self-worth and drive them to perform better. Here are some examples to illustrate the point.

> "Jamie, I've just monitored a half-dozen calls. What's with your opening statements? No two were even remotely alike! Come on, Jamie, you are one of the better reps here. You know what to do, and you know you can do better than that!"

> "Okay, Doug, what's going on? You know how to deliver your presentations better than most in the department. Your last few presentations were fragmented and disjointed, and it

shows in your results. You're better than that, and you know it!"

"Amanda, your handling of objections has gone from great to, well, poor. You know how to respond to these objections. You've been one of the best—a master. I expect more from you, and I think you expect more from yourself. Get back to form!"

"Pat! What's up? You had the client ready to bite, and you didn't bother to ask for the sale. And this is not the first time. I don't get it. Rookie reps have sat with you because you've always been the best at getting a commitment. Give your head a shake, and go back to what made you successful."

There is a bit of *"rah, rah, sis, boom, bah"* in this type of Vince Lombardi feedback, but it is calculated and deliberate. Remember, this is for successful reps who are faltering. You have *chosen* this approach because repeated attempts at using Socratic feedback have not been successful.

Use this approach wisely and carefully. It can be damaging if it is not used properly. You will note that most reps will usually become sullen because you bruised their ego. Some will get annoyed and lament to others around them. But at the heart of it, you nailed them where it counts—their egos. The majority will usually come around and get back to the good habits and standards that were set.

CHAPTER SIX

Other Approaches to Coaching

As the manager, you don't always have to be the coach. The fact of the matter is you won't always be there to coach on a consistent and ongoing basis. Fortunately, there are other ways to approach coaching and derive the same benefits.

In this Chapter

- Self-Coaching
- Blue sheet reporting
- The 10-2-5 chart
- Daily Flash meeting
- Buddy and mentor coaching
- The player coach

Self-Coaching

What is self-coaching?

Self-coaching is a bit misleading. Self-coaching is really a means of getting your reps to take greater personal responsibility for their sales activities and results. In effect, when they recognize that their activities and results are not achieving the goals, you want them to raise their hands and say, "Hey, I could use some help here." It's not unlike going to a doctor when you realize you have an ailment that won't go away.

You could also call this *personal accountability*.

By teaching your reps to become more personally accountable for their results, you are teaching them to proactively diagnose themselves. That way, you don't have to spend as much time and effort in the trenches. It means spending less time poring over sales reports at the end of the month.

When your sales team understands what the numbers mean, they can take the initiative to change their behavior. In some cases, they will go back to the basics—the standards that you set for skills and techniques—on their own and modify their behavior without your intervention. This is the ideal situation, the perfect scenario. In other cases, they will come to you and say, "I need your help, and here's where I am having problems." This will save you and your reps a ton of grief.

Self-awareness of activities and results can also be a powerful motivator. Seeing their sales efforts in real time (rather than at the end of the week or the month) can spur reps to work harder or smarter or both. Posting not-so-great results on a huge dry-erase board can be awkward and uncomfortable. That slight knock to the ego may be enough to get the rep to perform to-standard and achieve results. In a similar manner, reporting a tremendous day in front of a jury of your peers in a daily meeting can be a real ego booster. Pride is a great motivator and can push a rep to continue the positive behavior.

The 3 elements of self-coaching

The key to self-coaching is awareness. By making your telesales reps more aware of what they are doing, in terms of activities and results, they can quickly determine what they must do to either succeed or maintain their success.

Over the years, I borrowed (but mostly stole) and tested a number of great ideas and methods from various clients including blue sheet reporting, daily flash meetings and the 10-2-5 chart. Each of these elements listed below have been pillaged from successful companies and managers. By putting the three of them together, you have a process that is extremely powerful and effective in making your reps more aware of their own efforts and getting them to take action to improve results.

Blue Sheet Reporting

Blue sheet reporting has been around for decades. A blue sheet is simply a manual—yes, manual—tracking sheet that logs the activities and results of telesales reps in half-hour increments. The rep keeps an ongoing tally using a lumberman's (stickman) count. Here's an example.

Blue Sheet Example

Time	Dials	Propsect DMC	Client DMC	Sale	Value	Quote	Lead
8:00- 8:30							
8:30-9:00							
9:00-9:30							
9:30-10:00							
10:30-11:00							
11:00-11:30							
11:30-12:00							
12:00-12:30							
12:30-1:00							
1:00-1:30							
1:30-2:00							
2:00-2:30							
2:30-3:00							
3:00-3:30							
3:30-4:00							
4:00-4:30							
4:30-5:00							

Manual tracking? Are you kidding me?

I know what you're thinking. Why have the reps spend the time tracking the results when the software or telephone system or both can manage the task?

Two reasons. First, the time it takes to track results is minuscule. It takes less than one second for a rep to make a tiny mark on a sheet of paper. It does not take any time at all, so don't fall victim to that argument.

Second, telephone technology and software can provide you with some reports on dials, talk time, and the like. CRM software can provide you with sales and sales revenue. And if you have the time, you can marry one report with the other and plough through the information. You can even distribute it to your reps at the end of the week or month—whenever you run it—and hope they sort through it and read it. But it's not going to happen. You know it, and I know it.

Sure, manual tracking is a little old-fashioned and perhaps a little tedious, but it's highly effective in creating personal responsibility and accountability. The reps must record their activities in real time in half-hour segments. At any given point, you and your rep know precisely what has been accomplished.

Candidly, most sales reps don't like the blue sheets because they complain that it takes too much time and effort. Not true. They don't like the sheets because they create a conscience. That's why they're so darn effective. One of the prime reasons why reps are not as successful as they could be is because they stop doing the fundamentals, such as dialing and staying the course. The blue sheet reminds them, and it sometimes creates discomfort which motivates them to take action.

Why blue?

Put your tracking sheets on a colored sheet of paper. It can be blue, gray, or chartreuse for all I care. A colored sheet stands out on a desk. When you walk through your department, a quick glance will tell you if the rep is tracking or not. A blue sheet also makes it easier for you to find it and review it as you monitor by walking around

What a blue sheet does for you

But the blue sheets are more than just a check-and-balance job aid. For you, the blue sheet is means of quickly gauging the activity of your telesales reps and getting a pulse on what they are doing (or not doing).

For example, if a rep slips into a slump, instead of spending the time and effort monitoring calls to assess the situation, start by grabbing a handful of blue sheets and creating a hypothesis. This will save you loads of time. If the dial rate is low, you can probably bet it's simply an issue of a little more effort. But suppose the dial rate is high, but the decision-maker contact rate is low. What does that mean? Is the rep just unlucky, or maybe she's having a problem getting past the gatekeeper? This is where you begin your monitoring. If the contact rate is good but the sale rate has dropped, maybe the rep has begun to cut corners when questioning, or maybe the presentation has been diluted over time. Here's where you begin your call review.

How to get your telesales reps to do a blue sheet analysis

The blue sheet is more than just a recording tool; it's an analysis tool.

What makes the sheet so powerful is that your telesales reps are responsible not just for recording the key activities, but also they must total and analyze them by determining some key ratios. Here's how you do it.

Tally the totals.

At the end of every day, the reps are responsible for totalling the columns. They have to take a few seconds to count their stickmen and total the number of dials, connects, sales, and whatever else you decide is vital to track.

The mere fact that they are interacting with the blue sheets and tallying the numbers accomplishes certain things.

- First, the reps actually see what they accomplished during the day. They become conscious of the net results.
- Second, they do this at the end of every day. This means they know where they stand relative to their objectives. They know what they may need to do the following day. This beats the heck out of getting a report at the end of the week and sifting through the data.

Do the ratios.

The next thing your reps do before they pack up and head home is a ratio analysis. Your ratios may vary, but here are a few examples to illustrate the process.

- Contact rate = dials to connects (measures the ratio of dials to connects). Take the total number of connects (i.e., decision-maker contacts), and divide by the total number of dials. For example, if a rep made 60 dials and reached 25 decision makers, the contact rate is about 42 percent ($25 \div 60$).
- Sales rate = connects to sales (leads, appointments etc.). (Measures the ratio of contacts to sales). Take the total number of connects, and divide it into the total number of sales. For

example, if a rep makes 6 sales out of the 25 decision-maker connects, the sales rate is 24 percent (6 ÷ 25).

- Average Value of a Sale measures the average value of sale. Take the total value of all sales (i.e., total dollar value) and divide it by the number of sales made. For example, if a rep made 6 sales amounting to $15,314.36, the average value of a sale is $2,552.39 ($15,314.35 ÷ 6).

You get the idea. Again, the power of the exercise is getting the rep to do the math because it creates awareness. In turn, this creates personal accountability.

What's in it for you?

But for you, this process is extremely beneficial. If your reps are doing the tallies and the analysis, it means you don't have to. You save time and energy by getting the reps to self-report. All you need to do is sit back and observe (see the 10-2-5 chart) and listen (Flash reports). If something is out of whack, you can respond immediately. Your coaching does not have to wait for the end of the week, or more likely, the end of the month, when the software spits out the results.

But there's more to it.

If you take these results and enter them into a master spreadsheet that records the results of your sales team, you can quickly use the data to identify a baseline. In turn, you can use the data to draw comparisons of a rep's results relative to the team. This provides a degree of objectivity and perspective. In addition, you can use the numbers for forecasting and developing goals and objectives.

What about a good old-fashioned spread sheet?

Speaking of spreadsheets, should you create a spreadsheet so your reps can use it to tally the data and perform the analysis?

Nope—don't do it.

First and foremost, hot keying from a spreadsheet on a computer to an account or prospect screen *does* take time. But more significantly, a spreadsheet on the computer will likely be forgotten compared to an ugly blue (or chartreuse) sheet of paper sitting on the desk, forever reminding the reps to complete it.

Finally, the power of the blue sheet process is the *doing*. The reps are required to look at the results at the end of the day. Then they are required to interact with the data by counting the little tic marks. They have to grab a calculator and input the data. All these activities require attention and focus. They blatantly remind the reps of what they achieved and what they didn't achieve.

Introducing the blue sheets

The most important thing from a coaching perspective is to communicate, teach, instruct, and coach your reps on the benefits of keeping score. By pointing out that the blue sheets can be used to help them succeed in selling (and make more money), they can start using the sheets to do self-analysis and take action. If a rep sees that his close rate is dropping, he can take action, either on his own initiative or yours.

Why you might be tricked into *not* using a blue sheet.

Blue sheets are so old-fashioned and seemingly unsophisticated that you might be tempted not to use them. Don't get suckered into that train of thought. The blue sheets are deceptively simple, but in no way does that lessen their impact.

How you get your reps to comply

From the point of view of your telesales reps, doing a blue sheet is perceived as annoying. They *will* resist it. Or, they will forget.

You will get compliance by implementing a 10-2-5 chart and by conducting daily flash meetings.

The 10-2-5 Chart

The second element of self-coaching is the 10-2-5 chart. It's not particularly sophisticated but sometimes the simplest ideas are the best. The 10-2-5 chart is one of those ideas. Not only does it allow you to monitor the activities of your telesales team, but also it allows your telesales reps to monitor themselves and become more accountable for their results.

A 10-2-5 chart is typically a large dry-erase board that is prominently displayed within your telesales department. It features the names of your telesales reps and key indicators regarding productivity and sales, such as dials, connects, number of sales, value of sales, average value of sales, etc.

The 10-2-5 Chart

	10:00					2:00					5:00				
	Dials	DMCs	Sales	Total	Ave	Dials	DMCs	Sales	Total	Ave	Dials	DMCs	Sales	Total	Ave
Nikki	20	8	2	$400	$200	38	20	6	$3630	$605	47	28	9	$5481	$609
Zack	19	10	1	$1200	$1200	30	15	3	$3030	$1010	42	21	5	$5510	$1102
Amanda	27	11	4	$1628	$407	41	14	4	$1628	$407	46	15	4	$1628	$407
Craig	30	15	5	$5025	$1005	47	22	8	$7264	$908	67	28	10	$12.000	$1200
Beth															
John															

How it works and why it is brilliant

There's nothing new about a display chart, but what makes the 10-2-5 unique (and brilliant) is that at 10:00 am, 2:00 pm, and 5:00 pm your telesales reps have to get up from their desks and walk over to the chart and enter their stats.

For this little exercise, the reps use their blue sheets to calculate the results for those specific times. Think about this for a minute. The rep has to take about five minutes to count the stickman and total the amounts. This mere act gives the rep a real time look at his or her sales activities throughout the day. Next, the rep has to take those figures, walk to the board, and post his or her results.

It is big, bold, and brassy and there for everyone to see. Put these two activities together, and you compound awareness. The more they are aware of how they are doing, the harder they might work. They might also recognize they need some coaching.

It doesn't take a genius to see what's working here.

What the 10-2-5 does for the telephone rep

- It creates a sense of personal accountability for his or her own personal success.
- It creates a degree of pressure to perform if numbers are low.
- It creates a sense of pride and achievement if numbers are high.
- It creates a sense of good competition to drive the reps to work harder or smarter.
- It can act as an early warning indicator that the rep can recognize and seek help if necessary.

What it does for you, the manager or owner or executive

- It provides you with a real-time pulse of what is going on within your department.
- It acts as an early warning system for reps who may be faltering; in effect, you can nip a minor issue in the bud before it becomes major.
- It tells others in your company precisely what your department is doing.
- It does all this, and it holds *you* accountable, too!

5 Tips on How to build an effective 10-2-5 chart

There are some subtle, psychological elements at work with the 10-2-5 chart, and you want to leverage them. Here's how to make this simple idea yield bigger results.

1. Communicate the purpose of the chart.

Don't hold back. Tell your reps you *are* creating personal accountability and that you *will* be using it as a coaching tool. Emphasize the benefits.

Explain that you won't clobber someone if the numbers are down—that's part of selling—but that you will respond if numbers stay down. Make sure they see how the chart can help them!

2. Make the chart large.

Buy a gigantic dry-erase board. Or buy two and plunk them together. The chart must be obnoxiously visible for all to see. The stats that the reps enter will be blatantly evident to everyone from a great distance. Believe me, a rep who may have been slacking will be conscious of the results, and he or she will work harder. A rep who is doing well will beam with pride.

3. Make sure the reps report to the chart on time.

The idea is to pull the reps together at specified times, so it creates a group session—a jury of your peers, so to speak. They can cheer good results. They can feel pride if the numbers are great. They can feel sheepish, angry, or competitive if they are not great. Be tenacious about this. This is not an optional exercise. It tells everyone that activity and results are *important*.

4. Use the chart for motivation or incentives.

Create a prize for the top performers at 10:00, 2:00, and 5:00. Something small. A trophy. Have some fun with it. Or create a prize for the biggest percent increase between each time. Use the information from the chart to target and direct activities.

5. Monitor the chart.

The chart is there for you, too. Remember that. Glance at it every time you walk by. Make sure your reps are complying. If there are dips, note them, or check in with the rep. If you see a trend, respond accordingly. Monitor calls; begin the feedback process. Let your team know that you use the chart, too.

Why I hate fancy flat screens for reporting—and why you should, too.

The really hip thing that a lot of companies are doing now is using flat screen TVs to communicate messages and, more significantly, communicate the results on the floor. Typically, data is automatically gathered and fed to the screen for the world to see.

I hate them, and so should you. They're fancy (and often costly) but ineffective. I hate them because, after the second or third day, no one looks at them. The novelty is gone and the big screen becomes part of the wallpaper.

But the real reason why screens lose their impact is because the rep plays no part in the reporting process. Like a spreadsheet posted somewhere or passed around with the hope that reps will anxiously leaf through it, flat screen reporting does not encourage interaction.

Another thing is that the numbers silently change on the screen. From ten feet away, no one can read the individual numbers (which are usually in minuscule font), so they don't spur the reps on to greater and better calling. Unless you crowd around and squint, not much is achieved in terms of the benefits listed.

You have to make reporting a big deal, and you do that by making the reps responsible. Get them involved. Get them tracking. Get them calculating. Get them posting. Get them waiting behind the reps in front of them who are using the marker to list results. These are interactive activities that create awareness *and* impact behavior.

The 10-2-5 chart is perhaps one of the most *effective* recommendations I make to clients. It is so deceptively simple that it is almost too easy to dismiss. Don't be fooled. When implemented properly and combined with the blue sheets, it is a powerful driver of sales behavior. But there is one more element that completes the trifecta of self-coaching—the Flash reports.

Daily Flash Reports

Flash reports are something I picked up (okay, I stole it) from Becky Cruise, a telesales manager from the Midwest. It is a simple and extremely powerful coaching tool. I have since implemented it with virtually every company with whom I have worked.

What is Flash?

A Flash report is a quasi-reporting and coaching process which is designed to get telesales reps to collect their calling data (using the blue sheets) *and then publicly report* their results to peers and manager(s) at a daily meeting.

From a coaching perspective, a Flash report is relatively passive, but it creates a verbal conscience, whereby the reps must take personal *responsibility* and *accountability* for their selling activity and sales results. It creates a subtle degree of pressure to perform better because friends and co-workers are watching and listening. Many of your telephone reps will work that much harder to implement the skills and techniques that you have provided throughout the coaching process. No one wants to be embarrassed, and everyone wants to succeed.

Flash also gives you daily data on how your individual reps performed the day before. In effect, it can act as an early warning system if there is a dip in activity. You will always be up to date, which is critical when you get pressed for time. If something crops up, you can deal with it immediately and not let it fester out of control.

How it works

In a nutshell, Becky begins a process of personal accountability by having her reps keep a Daily Sales Report (DSR), her version of a blue sheet.

Each rep keeps track of key indicators by manually tracking outbound dials, customer contacts, inbound calls, direct sales, indirect sales, etc. Before the reps leave for the day, they put their DSR in a Flash folder on Becky's desk. The act of submitting a form tends to make the rep more conscious of his or her results. Knowing that the report will be reviewed pushes the rep to achieve better results.

The next morning, before dialing begins, Becky has her Flash meeting, which is stand-up affair attended by all the reps in her office. It only takes about fifteen minutes, and each rep reports his or her own individual results. For example, someone might say,

> "I had 20 calls for the day, 80 minutes on the phone, an
> average sale of $300, and I made 4 sales. I had new product
> or promo sales of 10 percent total dollars and no sales for the
> daily double."

In this example, the rep did not have a particularly good day. In contrast to what the rep announced, the average number of calls per day is 37 and the average minutes on the phone is 140. The average sale figure is $353, and the average total sales is 9. In the meeting, Becky will comment on the results and ask, "What was going on yesterday?"

The rep has an opportunity to explain. Sometimes there are legitimate reasons, and sometimes there are lame excuses. The interesting thing is that, after a period of time, the lame excuses eventually disappear, and the rep tends to speak more candidly about issues or problems (e.g., trouble overcoming objections). Sometimes they just fess up and say, "I blew it." This works because they know what needs to be done.

The meeting goes on. For instance, the next telesales rep might say,

> "I made 52 calls and was on the phone for 166 minutes, with an average sale value of $477. I made 12 sales, and new product sales amounted to 22 percent of the total dollars."

Obviously, this rep had a better day and very good results. From a coaching perspective, this is an opportunity to provide positive feedback in front of the rep's peers. Through the acknowledgment of this rep's superb results, the rep will be encouraged to work harder and smarter. Simple psychology.

Flash: the benefits

By publicly declaring their results in front of their boss and peers, a number of benefits occur for the reps and the team as a whole.

1. As mentioned earlier, if the rep has had a lousy day, there is a degree of discomfort in sharing the results with everyone else; but the stress is good stress because it tends to motivate the rep to work harder or smarter for the upcoming day. No one wants to report poor results two days in a row!
2. If the rep had a good day, it is an opportunity for him or her to shine and get a few high fives; it appeals to the rep's ego and pushes him or her to continue to perform well. It gives the

manager a chance to praise the rep, and typically fellow reps will chime in with praise.

3. When reps have had a bad day, their teammates tend to rally around them and give them verbal encouragement. They've all been there, and they know what it's like; so, in effect, it builds team spirit.

4. At any given moment, the rep knows exactly what is important, what is expected, and precisely where he or she stands; the results are big, bold, and brassy. There's no running or hiding or pretending if the results are mediocre or poor.

5. The manager immediately identifies good, mediocre, or poor results from the previous day. There is no waiting for a weekly report; it saves everybody time and energy.

6. The manager can immediately develop a plan of action for that individual—maybe it is coaching, or maybe it is training. Something can be done before the rep spirals and is lost.

Bonus benefit

Becky also attaches some sort of recognition or reward program with the Flash sessions. For instance, she has slips of paper on which she writes key statistics (e.g., dials, contacts, number of sales, highest sale, or average value of sale). A draw is made, and the person with the highest number in the selected category wins a small prize.

Flash is such a simple process to implement that there is no reason why you can't do it. In all my years of consulting and coaching, I have discovered that this is one of the *most* powerful ways to supplement the coaching effort. It acts as a wake-up call every morning and reminds reps of what they must do in order to be successful. Implement Flash today, and start seeing the results tomorrow.

Mentoring and Buddy Coaching

A second approach to coaching is the called mentoring or buddy coaching. Often seen in small companies (but is not infrequent in larger firms), a mentoring or buddy-coaching system is a method of providing informal guidance and coaching to rookie telesales reps by veteran telesales reps.

Benefits of mentors and buddy coaches

Mentors or buddy coaches help rookie reps integrate into the company or department. They work one-to-one with the reps on the sales floor, and they are available when the rookie needs help or direction. There are several benefits to a mentoring or buddy-coaching program.

1. It can save the sales manager considerable time and effort. Day-to-day instruction and guidance with any number of reps can be extremely time-consuming. Delegating to a buddy coach can free up time.

2. Not only does it save the manager's time, but also it saves the rookie's time as well. A quick question can be answered almost immediately by their mentor. The rookie doesn't have to wait until the manager is free and available for a question. This reduces frustration and stress.

3. Mentors and buddy coaches help the rookie integrate faster into the company or department. Because the program is more informal, they tend to learn the tricks of the trade faster. They meet others, make friends, learn the company culture, and get comfortable. Consequently, the rookie becomes more productive and profitable in a shorter amount of time.

4. A good mentoring or buddy-coaching system tends to make the veteran rep feel a greater sense of value. In some cases, being a mentor or a buddy coach is a perk. Many are paid a

small stipend for their efforts. It varies their jobs, making them more interesting.

The dangers of a mentor or buddy-coaching system

Despite the benefits of a mentoring or buddy-coaching system, there are some dangers to implementing the program.

1. A mentoring or buddy-coaching program can be extremely time-consuming for the mentor. Sales from your mentors and buddy coaches can take a dip. If they are spending time providing coaching and guidance, they are not spending time on sales. So a program like this might impact your bottom line.

2. A mentor can easily get annoyed and frustrated with the program. Often companies will introduce a mentoring program and expect the veterans to dedicate time and effort to grooming the rookie. But they won't make any adjustments to sales and revenue goals and objectives. The poor veteran will get stressed out trying to make the numbers while assisting the rookie. At some point, they begin to resent the program, the company, and the rookie. Who can blame them? As a result, the veterans tend to dilute the quality of their mentoring.

3. Similarly, if the buddy program affects the veteran's commission or bonus, the same resentment occurs. The mentoring can suffer accordingly.

4. Mentors may not actively support the specific skills, techniques, or processes that were taught in training. While working with a client in Florida, it was discovered that veterans were actively telling rookies, "Don't use that technique (e.g., opening statement). It doesn't work." The buddy coaches were not consciously trying to undermine the training. In fact, they thought they were helping the rookies by giving them the inside scoop. The trouble was, the rookie was left confused. Almost

immediately, they would use the veteran's techniques, but they didn't have the veteran's knowledge or savvy. The results for the rookies were invariably lousy.

Finally, many companies have multiple mentors rather than dedicated mentors. This means a rookie can go to one of any number of mentors for advice. One veteran might offer one suggestion, while another offers a different suggestion for the same issue. This can leave rookie reps completely confused. When calls are monitored, the poor rep has a hodgepodge of styles and techniques, none of which work.

Making a mentoring and buddy coaching system work for you

An effective mentoring and buddy-coaching system can be implemented and can do wonders for the development of your reps.

First, clearly define the role of the mentor.

If the mentor is supposed to provide basic guidance and direction, fine. But if the mentor's role is to actively provide coaching and development, give your buddy coaches formal coaching training. (Getting them to read this book might be a start.)

Second, clearly explain to the buddies that they must actively support and coach the skill standards defined in the training program even if the veteran does not adhere to them.

In the Florida example, the mentors learned to say something to this effect:

> "I use a different approach based on my experience and background. You will develop your own approach in time.

> But in the meantime, stick to what you learned in training. Master those techniques first."

This worked extremely well once it was implemented. Rookies stuck to the training standards, and the buddy coaches did not feel compromised.

Third, monitor your mentors.

Mentors need coaching on how to coach. Apply the same fundamentals to coaching that you apply to skills training. It's as simple as that. Make sure your mentors are adhering to the standards.

The Player Coach

The player coach is a hybrid of a telesales rep manager and a telephone sales rep. In other words, the player coaches are responsible for managing, developing, training, and coaching a sales team, and they are responsible for managing, developing, and generating revenues from an account or territory base.

The challenge

In a nutshell, the player coach is usually not an effective or successful arrangement. I have not seen it work effectively anywhere in the last twenty years. The player coach is invariably torn between the two responsibilities. Both tug away at the player coach, demanding attention and focus. It's a difficult act to balance.

Relative to coaching telephone reps, the challenge for a player coach is that the coaching becomes an "important, but not urgent" task. Player coaches are typically governed by whatever is urgent at the time; they put out fire after fire. If their clients demand action, they react. If sales are down, they focus on business development. If their commissions are taking a hit, they pick up the phones. If the boss is unhappy with results, they drop everything and call.

Guess what happens to coaching?

Coaching drops to the bottom of the must-do list. If coaching is missed for a day or two or three or more because the company has a month-end sales objective to meet, the world won't end. The player coach will try to save the day by cranking out additional sales.

Of course, the net result is that coaching doesn't get done with any regularity or consistency. When it does get done, it is usually diluted and ineffective. In the longer term, sales do not grow with any measured consistency because many of the reps are not selling to their potential. Turnover occurs because the telephone reps get frustrated by lack of success. Replacing them takes time. Money is spent on recruiting. Training is streamlined to get the new rep onto the phones. Coaching is ignored because the player coach is far behind. This is a cycle that I just don't like.

6 steps to implementing a player-coach program

Sometimes a player-coach program is the only alternative, especially for small companies with tight budgets. The company wants the direction and focus that a manager can bring to help develop the telephone reps, but it doesn't have the resources to dedicate a full-time manager to do the job.

You *can* make a player-coach program work, but it requires a plan and discipline. Here's how.

1. Clearly define the roles and responsibilities of the player coach. Write a job description. A job description takes time and effort, but it forces you to articulate and define the position. Apply percentages of time. For example, "Coaching (monitoring, analyzing, and providing feedback): 20%/day (approximately 1.5 hours per day)." Putting it in writing shows you're serious, and it beats the heck out of saying, "Coaching," which is vague and noncommittal.

2. Schedule the coaching sessions a week or two in advance. Block them out on the Outlook calendar. Share the calendar with your reps and your boss. Use color codes and set alarms. Treat the coaching appointment like you would treat a visit to a doctor; be serious about it.

3. Refuse to budge when conflicts occur. If your boss wants a meeting that conflicts with your coaching schedule, refuse the meeting, and offer an alternative.

4. Record the results of your coaching. It does not have to be complex or detailed, just something that holds you accountable. For example, "Monitored Janice for thirty minutes; applying standards consistently. Monitored Michelle and provided feedback on opening statements."

5. Submit the coaching report to the boss. Here is another level of accountability. If you're an owner or executive, this should be considered a mission-critical task and should be treated as such. Remember the old adage, "What gets measured, gets done." Simply knowing that someone will (or might) look at the report is a compelling reason to continue the coaching process.

6. Stay disciplined. The temptation to put the coaching aside for "just this one time" will assault you every day. Remember that coaching is like an exercise routine; you need to stick to it if you want to get and stay fit. Get into the routine and it becomes easier.

CONCLUSION

I s coaching the holy grail of making telephone sales reps more effective and successful?

No, of course not. There are other factors that contribute to sales success. But active, structured, one-to-one coaching comes pretty close.

Consistently applied coaching will do three things for your company and your reps. First, it will help your telephone sales reps sell smarter. Coaching will encourage them to properly use skills and techniques (standards) that work instead applying random and/or less effective tactics. Secondly, your telesales reps will sell better. Your coaching ensures consistency and compliance. The more they apply the skill sets, the better they'll get. Finally, if your reps sell smarter and better, you can be assured they'll sell more. And that's the name of the game.

If you're serious about sales results, you need to be serious about coaching. Nothing, absolutely nothing, will give you better results. Not even close.

Committing to coaching is committing to sales improvement.

ABOUT THE AUTHOR

Since 1993, Jim Domanski has been the president of Teleconcepts Consulting, helping business-to-business companies and individuals use the telephone more effectively to sell and market their products.

Cited by *Canadian Business Magazine* as "Canada's reigning tele-management guru," Jim is regarded as one of North America's foremost experts of outbound telesales and telephone support programs. He has pioneered some of the most innovative telesales strategies with a variety of companies in the US and Canada.

He has written three books, *Direct Line to Profits*, *Profiting by Phone*, and *Add-On Selling*. Jim has also written hundreds of articles and has been featured in numerous magazines and newspapers throughout North American, including *Marketing*, *Advertising Age*, *Selling Power*, *Sales and Marketing Management*, *Profit*, and the *Financial Post*. He has been interviewed on radio and television and has lectured at various universities and colleges. Jim writes and publishes two highly acclaimed weekly e-newsletters, *Tele-Sales Vitamins* and *Tele-Profiting*.

For ten years, Jim coached minor-league hockey and football. It was from these experiences that he derived many of the principles for coaching telesales reps.

As a trainer, consultant, and coach, he has worked with companies big and small throughout the US, Canada, and Europe.

For more information on Teleconcepts training and coaching programs, please visit www.telesalesmaster.com.

For information on consulting services, please visit www. teleconceptsconsulting.com or call 613-591-1998.

CPSIA information can be obtained at www.ICGtesting.com
Printed in the USA
LVOW13s1723240713

344448LV00009B/1044/P

9 781466 951792